ANCIENT PATHWAYS
IN THE
ALPS

Giovanni Caselli & Keith Sugden
Foreword by John Hillaby

D0533258

British Library Cataloguing in Publication Data

Caselli, Giovanni
    Ancient pathways in the Alps.
    1. Alps—Description and travel—Guide-books   2.
    Walking—Alps—Guide-books
    I. Title   II. Sugden, Keith
    914.94'70473   DQ823.5

    ISBN 0-540-01122-3
    © Giovanni Caselli and Keith Sugden 1988

Designed by Richard Souper

Maps by Nicholas Hewetson

Published by
George Philip and Son Limited,
27a Floral Street, London WC2E 9DP

Printed in Hong Kong

Front cover illustration: the Lucomagno Pass between cantons Graubünden and Ticino

Back cover illustration: Piedmontese peasants returning at eventide, painted from life near Lanzo by Estella Canziani in about 1910

Contents

FOREWORD BY JOHN HILLABY

On two occasions a distant view of the Alps, that enormous barrier between the warmth, the fertility of the Mediterranean and the wealth of north-western Europe, caused the small hairs on the nape of my neck to tingle, slightly.

On the first occasion, a week or two before I set off on a 1200-mile walk from the Netherlands to Nice, I saw that chaotic land mass from a DC10 which purred through the thin air two miles above the twisted shoulder of the Matterhorn. As far as the eye could see through a plastic porthole, there seemed neither grain nor pattern in the redundancy of snow-capped peaks and chisel-sharp defiles.

How would it feel to walk alone amidst topological confusion? The analogy of an ant moving slowly, diagonally across a huge sheet of corrugated cardboard came to mind with disturbing clarity.

On the second occasion – as I strode down from Neuchâtel to Lausanne – the Savoy Alps appeared to rise slowly, one after another, like mobile stage scenery above the death-grey water of Lake Geneva. Yet within a few days I learnt how to grapple with mountains with increasing confidence. The walk took just over two months to accomplish and there were few days when I did not feel on top of the world, not least because, through accident or design, I found myself among a huddle of seventeenth-century chalets whose occupants fingered the adjustable frame of my high-pack as if it were a hang-glider. That was nearly twenty years ago.

Today, the ancient wooden houses on stilts are being done up as *chalets modernes pour vacances*. Ski-villes reproduce themselves like waterweed. Bits break off; they float away and take root elsewhere. Package tourists are treated like parcels even to the point of being issued with addressed cards in case they get lost during brief time on their own.

My old friend and route-master, Giovanni Caselli, and his colleague, Keith Sugden, are offering us something entirely different, a mapped guide to the mountain routes of yesterday. Here is a book to be savoured, to be carried about and re-read at leisure for, unless they are mendicants or mad, people do not wander about in the Alps unless they enjoy it and know what to look for.

INTRODUCTION

View from Schloss Supersaxo over Naters and the Rhône valley. The prominent spire and Romanesque tower belong to the Catholic parish church of St Mauritius.

If for you the touchstone of travel is miles under your boots, stop here. Our way of travelling is an altogether more varied experience. Not for us the 'because it's there' walks of the alpinists; in our company you always journey with a theme from the past and, we trust, learn rather more than the person behind the wheel of the Mercedes-Benz.

Here you find history – living history in the traditions and ways of life of the mountain people. You will look in vain for details of hotels, specialities in food and wine, postbus routes and ski-lifts. Such information is found in other guides, all freely available on the spot if not in advance.

Each of the six ancient pathways we describe explores a different theme. 'The Swiss Alps' and 'The Italian Alps and Lakes' juxtapose the central fastnesses with those cultures which face the Mediterranean world, while 'The Amber Route' crosses the whole chain from north to south.

'The Roman Roads of Noricum' explores the Austrian Alps from a point near the Yugoslav border. By contrast a traditional peasant way of life is found along 'The Drove Roads of Provence'.

Perhaps the most satisfying of all is 'The Waldensians' Glorious Return', for in this walk you cross the mountains in the tracks of a Protestant band – to find at the end of it that

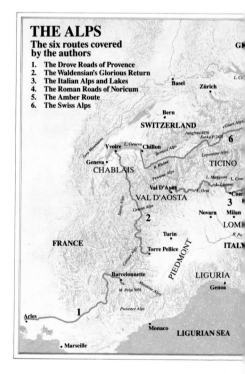

THE ALPS
The six routes covered by the authors

1. The Drove Roads of Provence
2. The Waldensian's Glorious Return
3. The Italian Alps and Lakes
4. The Roman Roads of Noricum
5. The Amber Route
6. The Swiss Alps

three centuries later the descendants of those
zealous refugees are waiting to welcome you to
their valleys.

Each ancient pathway has its own introduction to help you choose the route to follow.
Widely spread in theme, period and geography,
our routes also vary in the methods of transport
which can be used to follow them. For the
Glorious Return and the Swiss Alps feet are
highly recommended. For the Amber Route and
the Roman Roads of Noricum bicycles are a
practical alternative. For the other two a
mixture of methods might be better.

The Romantic movement of Napoleonic times
was a turning point in people's attitude towards
the Alps. In England mountain-worship
featured in the writings and drawings of the
youthful John Ruskin so that, by the time he first
glimpsed the Alps in 1833 during a European
tour with his parents, he was ecstatic:

At the geographical centre of
the Alps, looking west from the
Furka Pass across the infant
Rhône to the Grimsel Pass and
Grimsel See

> It was drawing towards sunset, when
> we got up to some sort of garden
> promenade – west of Schaffhausen, I
> believe – suddenly – behold – beyond!
>
> There was no thought in any of us
> for a moment of their being clouds.
> They were clear as crystal, sharp on
> the pure horizon sky, and already
> tinged with rose by the sinking sun.
> Infinitely beyond all that we had ever
> thought or dreamed – the seen walls of
> lost Eden could not have been more
> beautiful to us; nor more awful, round
> heaven, the walls of sacred Death. . . .

THE DROVE ROADS OF PROVENCE

In the footsteps of the flocks

As summer approaches you may see in many parts of the world sturdy shepherds trudging up steep trails, driving herds of sheep towards the mountain meadows. If you pass that way again when the first chill winds of autumn are tumbling the leaves from the trees, you will meet those same shepherds herding the flocks down to the lowland grazing grounds. This practice of moving animals – cattle and goats as well as sheep – between winter pastures in the lowlands and summer pastures in the highlands is called transhumance.

While a farmer in the English Cotswolds or the western hills of France might never need to

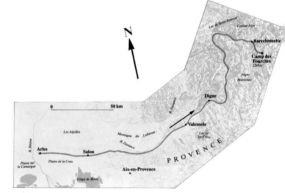

move his flock to different heights, in less temperate climates transhumance is a pressing necessity, and nowhere more so than in the valleys and mountain slopes of the Alps. For by May the grass in the plain and valley pastures withers to brown stalks which provide no nourishment, and by October the luscious mountain grasslands are covered by thick snow which may lie for as long as seven months.

The epicurean sheep cannot easily be persuaded to partake of dried hay like other domesticated beasts, and so in Europe the obvious tactic of moving flocks to the green grass developed around 4000 years ago. Modern research has shown that by adopting transhumance these early farmers were unconsciously giving a Vitamin A benefit to their sheep.

The shepherd may establish his family in a settled home either near the winter plains or close to the mountain pastures. Occasionally home will be in an intermediate village. In the French Alps, which concern us here, the transhumance is predominantly ascending – in other words, the shepherds are based in the plains. Recent German research has shown that ninety-two per cent of the shepherds live around the winter pastures of Provence in La Crau, a pebbly area of the Rhône delta east of Arles, which in summer turns into a burning semi-desert as the grass withers between the hot stones.

The ancient drove road of the Crau shepherds between Vignon-sur-Verdon and St-Grégoire

From La Crau the traditional drove roads radiate north to the high plateau of Vercors, and north-east to the mountain pastures along the Italian border between Briançon and Barcellon-ette. The shepherds may rent different pastures for their flocks each summer, but whichever pastures they use they will always find a remote cabin, or perhaps a group of cabins, for their accommodation. In one high valley approaching Col de la Moutière, south of Barcellonette, we saw what at first appeared to be a Stone Age settlement. It turned out to be a set of quite recent foundations for shepherds' cabins, arranged in a circle with paths radiating from a communal fireplace in the centre.

Until the Second World War most of the flocks did the whole 300km (185 miles) journey on foot. But since 1950 rail transport from St-Martin-de-Crau station or travelling the roads by truck have become more usual, and some practicable roads now lead right into the remote mountain pastures.

A few flocks still walk all the way, but they are spread over so many different routes that you will be lucky to see one. Where the shepherds are obliged to use motor roads the problems they face in preventing 2000 sheep from wandering off the road to eat someone else's tempting pasture, while at the same time trying to usher impatient traffic through safely, can easily be imagined.

A traditional transhumance in the French Alps might typically consist of 2500 sheep with just a few goats. At the head of the flock comes the leading shepherd with his dog, whose job is to keep up a steady pace of 3km/h (less than 2mph). If you greet the shepherd he is unlikely to stop while replying, because he will not want to break the slow rhythm of the march.

Spaced at intervals down the line are three more shepherds with their dogs. Their task is to keep the sheep on the straight and narrow, and off the juicy green shoots in wayside fields and vineyards. There has been plenty of friction over the centuries between sheep and settled arable farmers, and that is a tradition most shepherds do not want to keep up! Bringing up the rear of the procession is a fifth shepherd, with his dog. Their task is to prevent stragglers from falling behind.

Three donkeys are an essential part of the team. Two of these beasts carry large, evenly laden panniers, tightly strapped to prevent their slipping, while the third donkey pulls a cart carrying the heaviest domestic equipment and any members of the flock or escort who may be injured or fall sick on the journey. The shepherds take with them as much as possible of the many items they will need while living far from shops, from sheep medicine to needles and thread.

The flock travels 30km (19 miles) a day in two marches of five hours, with a long break in between for rest and refreshment to avoid walking in the midday sun. This pattern means that camp is struck before dawn and the day's march begins as early as five in the morning. The shepherds, who know the route well, head for regular, well-watered pastures at noon and overnight. For a direct and witty eye-witness account of a transhumance on foot written by an Alpine shepherd, we recommend Henri Chassillan's booklet *La Transhumance: témionage vécu*, published in 1985 by Marcel Petit of Raphèle-lès-Arles.

Once in the mountain pastures the flock is split into groups; each little flock can be controlled by one shepherd. Lambs may be separated from their mothers, and towards autumn the rams will be isolated so as to control breeding. During this pastoral idyll (for the sheep) the shepherds are hard at work moving the flocks, repairing fences and gathering wood for the fire. Once a week one or two of them make a provisioning expedition to the nearest large village or market town to buy bread, fruit, vegetables and medicine. This is often on a regular day of the week, so that shepherds from neighbouring pastures have an opportunity to meet, exchange gossip and swap novels.

It is a curious fact that sheep are not raised along most of the Alpine chain. In the Italian,

A French shepherd's donkey cart drawn from a *c*1950 photograph

Swiss and Austrian Alps cattle are the main livestock. We find sheep only in the French Alps, then continuing round on the slopes facing the Mediterranean Sea through the Ligurian mountains into the Apennines. The traditional culture and costumes of the shepherds bear close similarities all the way from Provence through Liguria to Tuscany.

The sheep raised in Provence are mainly Rambouillets of the mixed Merino type. They are a fine-woolled breed which take their name from the French national experimental farm at Rambouillet, near Paris, where they were first bred. The brown Ligurian sheep are thought to be descended from Bronze Age stock.

What is the economic value of these Provençal sheep? Traditionally they were kept only for the production of milk, cheese and wool. None of them was killed except for a ritually slaughtered lamb at Easter. However, during the twentieth century meat production has become a significant economic part of Provençal sheep-rearing.

Of the many drove roads which radiate from La Crau into the French Alps we have chosen the one leading into the Ubaye Valley for three reasons. It is believed to be among the oldest (in one place it follows a deserted stretch of the Roman Via Aurelia); it offers the opportunity of pleasant travelling; and the final pastures of the Champs des Fourches are near Barcellonette, itself a most engaging market town for a stay in the mountains. The Champs des Fourches lie more than 2400m (8000 feet) above sea level.

We planned that this route would be one for walkers, to follow, albeit more briskly, in the footsteps of the flocks. There is no reason why it cannot be enjoyed by cyclists, but if the exact route is followed it will involve some rough riding, as well as the negotiation of ditches and fences.

Arles and the Museon Arletan

Arles was a town of the Ligurian tribe when Julius Caesar founded there the colony of Arelate to house retired army veterans from the Sixth Legion. Being then much closer to the coast than it is today, it also flourished as a naval and commercial port. Surviving from that period are a 7000-seat theatre and the largest amphitheatre north of the Alps.

From 879 to 1150 Arles was the capital of the Kingdom of Burgundy. It was later disputed by the German emperors, the counts of Provence and the kings of France. The town then sank into comparative obscurity, and in 1944 it was badly bombed.

The magnificently sculptured portal (1190) of the former cathedral of St Trophime dominates the Place de la République and leads into one of the best Romanesque churches in Provence. The Museon Arletan in the Rue de la République was founded by the Provençal poet Frédéric Mistral in 1896; eight

[Map showing the area around Arles with locations including: Les Gr. des Terres, Mas des Pommiers, Augery, Ledignan, Fourques, L'Île des Sables, Le Grand Rhône, Les Templiers, Montplaisin, Portagnel, Mas de Vert, Tête de la Camargue, Trinquetaille, Arles, Le Petit Clar, Mas Pilles, M, Chantiers Navals de Barriol, Beauchamp, Mas de Baou, Pont de Grau, Mas de Musc, Canal d'Arles, Fourchon, Gagnon, Institut Medico Professionnel. Scale: 0 1 2km. N (north arrow).]

years later he devoted to the project his Nobel Prize for literature. Housed in the sixteenth-century Hôtel de Laval-Castellane, it illustrates local history, customs, costume and crafts. Shepherds and their way of life are well represented, for example by a reconstructed shepherd's hut.

The ruined Roman theatre at Arles

A nineteenth-century monument to Provence at Arles

A shepherd of La Crau, drawn in 1910

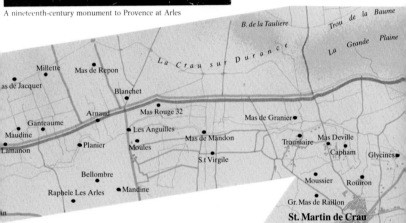

La Crau: the Stony Plain

La Crau is the name of a wide plain of pebbles in the valley of the River Rhône where the sheep winter. The dispersion of these water-borne pebbles in the Rhône basin is a recent geological event, resulting from the melting of glaciers in the Alpine valleys. Indeed, until the not-too-distant past the Camargue, the marshy grassland in the Rhône delta, was a gulf of the Mediterranean and the delta continues to grow at the expense of the sea.

The nineteenth-century English travel writer Augustus Hare (1834–1903) travelled through La Crau on a train from Arles to Salon in 1890, observing:

The Muséon Arletan founded by Frédéric Mistral in 1904

Soon after leaving Arles, the railway enters the vast, weird, wind-tormented plain of *La Crau*, the *Campus Lapidus* of the Romans, covered with stones. Here Hercules, returning from Iberia, is supposed to have been stopped by two giants, Albion and Bergion, sons of Neptune, and Jupiter came to his rescue by crushing them with a shower of stones.

Whichever theory you favour for the origin of the pebbles, a visit in summer is likely to be both oppressive from the dry heat and impressive from the solitude: not a sheep to be seen. The area of natural semi-desert is now, however, much smaller than it used to be, for irrigation schemes over the past century have brought many parts of La Crau under cultivation.

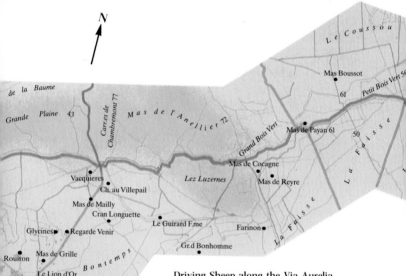

Driving Sheep along the Via Aurelia

It will be seen from the map that there is a completely straight length of drove road running for some 6km (4 miles) south-east to Le Merle, now a French agricultural college. This is an abandoned section of the Roman Via Aurelia between the important cities of Aquae Sextiae (now Aix-en-Provence) and Avennio (Avignon) on the River Rhône.

Aquae Sextiae was founded during the Roman Republic when the much older Greek trading colony of Massalia (Roman Massilia; modern Marseilles) came

The stony plain of La Crau near Le Merle in July

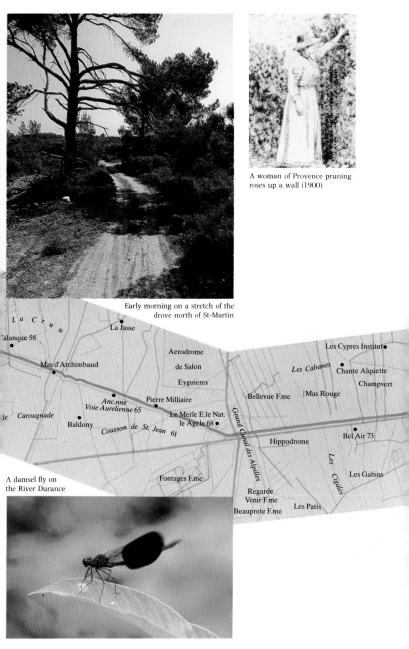

A woman of Provence pruning roses up a wall (1900)

Early morning on a stretch of the drove north of St-Martin

A damsel fly on the River Durance

under attack from the Salluvii tribe. In 124 BC the Roman consul Sextius Calvinus led an expedition into Gaul and defeated the Salluvii. To prevent a recurrence of the trouble he built a fort in their territory and named it after himself.

Judging from its local name the Via Aurelia was built on instructions from the Emperor Aurelian and therefore dates from the period of his reign, AD 270–275. As it heads towards the edge of the stony plain of La Crau this level road is flanked by two lateral drainage ditches. These ditches are still maintained and restrict access to the central strip. Consequently the old road surface is choked with dense undergrowth which mostly constrains walkers to the parallel path.

A street in Salon-de-Provence

Salon-de-Provence and Nostradamus

Augustus Hare described Salon-de-Provence as it was in Victorian days in *South-Eastern France*:

> *Salon.* The church of *S. Laurent* contains the tomb of the famous astrologer, Michel de Nostradamus, *ob.* 1566. The favourite of Catherine de Médicis, he was visited here by Charles ɪx. His poet-son César erected the bust upon his tomb inscribed – *Clarissimi ossa Michaelis Nostrodami unius omnium mortalium judicio digni, cujus pene divino calamo, totius orbis, ex astronum inflexu futuri eventus conscriberentur.* [This rather corrupt Latin can be translated: 'The bones of the very famous Michel de Notredame, the one, in the judgement of all mortals, by whose almost divine pen the future events of the whole world have been described from the influence of celestial bodies.']

Salon formerly stood on the edge of the Crau, now separated from it by richly

The castle at Salon-de-Provence, called L'Emperi

cultivated land fertilized by the waters of the Durance, supplied through the *Canal de Crapponne*, named after its creator, Adam de Crapponne.

There is now a small museum devoted to Nostradamus and his credulous patrons in what was his house near the church of St Michel.

Hare failed to mention the vast château of L'Emperi,

which has twelfth-century fortifications, an entrance gateway rebuilt in 1585 and a seventeenth-century guardhouse. The castle houses the *Musée National d'Art et d'Histoire Militaire*. Today Salon is best known for the fact that it is the training headquarters for French Air Force officers.

A French shepherd's mobile cabin drawn from a *c*1950 photograph

Sunflowers growing along the drove road

Vines growing near Lambesc

A Provençal Poet

Among the early students of European folk culture was the Provençal poet Frédéric Mistral, who founded the Museon Arletan in 1896. He wrote the following dedicatory sonnet in the local dialect and in French for *Le Costume en Provence* (1907) by his friend Juli Charle-Roux. If the Provençal seems to have a large dose of Italian in it, remember that Nice was Italian until Count Camillo di Cavour bargained away his homeland to secure French support for the *Risorgimento*, the unification of Italy in the nineteenth century.

Actibus immensis urbs fulget massiliensis
De ti Paire as rendu vivènto la deviso:
 l'Empéri dou Soulèu, bèl ome, à toun aflat
dins Marsiho faguè trelusi soun esclat
sus touti li nacioun que la grand mar diviso.

E vuei poulidamen toun cor d'or soulenniso
l'engèni prouvençau e, coume lou sant blad
qu'en taulo de Calèndo espelis sus lou plat,
dins ti record pious nosto Prouvènço niso.

The public fountain in Rognes

A placid stretch of the River Durance from the bridge at Pertuis

N'aguessian quauquis-un, fort e bon coume tu,
e veirian dou pais regreia la vertu,
lis art sagatèja sus nosto roucassiho.

L'oulivié patriau flouca lou terradou
e lou mounde crida souto l'Amiradou:*
≪ Toustems per si grand-fa resplendigue
    Marsiho. ≫

                    *

Tu as rendu vivante la devise de tes pères:
L'empire de soleil, sous tes auspices, bel ami,
Fit briller son éclat dans Marseille, sur toutes
Les nations que la grand mer divise.

Gentiment aujourd'hui, ton coeur d'or solennise
La génie provençal: et comme le blé saint
Qui germe sur la table et le plat de Noël,
Notre Provence gite dans les souvenirs pieux.

En eussions-nous quelques-uns, forts et bons
Comme toi. Nous verrions du pays revivre
La vertu, les beaux-arts drageonner sur nos
    rochers arides.

L'olivier patriote couronner le terroir
Et le monde crier devant l'Amiradou:*
≪ Par ses actes immenses Marseille
    resplendit. ≫

*The *Amiradou* is a quay in Marseilles from which
people used to observe the arrival of ships.

Poppies along the drove road

The Other Drove Roads of Provence

While following this drove road let us not forget that we are heading for just one possible high-altitude pasture of many in the French Alps. From the winter plains in La Crau the shepherds traditionally move their flocks to a region about 160km (100 miles) long, between the Isère valley far up the River Rhône and Nice on the coast. The drove roads divide into two: the one that leads north up the Rhône and the set of parallel routes that start by heading east from Arles.

Northwards there is but one destination, the high limestone plateau of Vercors between Valence and Grenoble. Until recently it was one of the wildest regions of France. The landscape is broken up by mountain ridges and deep valleys. It is featured in the book *La Transhumance*, where Marie Mauron describes the shepherds' summer existence in a rather romantic style.

The other traditional drove roads all go roughly east to the vicinity of Valensole, where they diverge widely to reach the pastures which feed the various tributaries of the River Durance. This is not to say that the flocks follow the rivers all the way to the

Epur

Le Puy S.te Reparade

Les Iscles

Perroquet

Les Goirands   Les Grottes

Les Merles

La Quille St. Reparade

La Prise 195

Le Logis Neuf

La Mazouillette

Gronle 209   La Bastide Neuve   196

Fonscolombe Ch.au

Repentance Ch.au

D15

Les Éscabins

Laumartin F.me 199

La P.te te Bastide   Bailie

N

Meyragues   La Cadenière   St. Payre   Quartier de la

Recuelles

La Grange   St. Epur

M.gne de Maringas 454   Le Perrou F.me

Campagnerose

Le D

Forêt c

An example of the profuse wild flowers along the drove road in summe

mountains. As we know from our route, the shepherds often prefer to cross or follow ridges, because in this way they avoid the difficulties of travelling through the more heavily settled valleys. But as the sheep journey 30km (19 miles) a day and must have a midday rest and grazing stop, a drove road should descend every 15km (9 miles) to suitable pasture by a stream.

A Provençal peasant woman with a wheelbarrow (1900)

Our destination at Champs des Fourches is on the eastern side of the mountain pastures reached by the Durance routes. They stretch from Briançon in the north, to Serres in the west and to Col de Luens on the Route Napoléon in the south. Imagine the joy of being a sheep in all those endless luscious pastures in July!

The War Memorial at St-Paul-les-Durance

The Costume of Provence

The study and revival of Provençal costume in the twentieth century owes much to the Provençal poet and folklorist Frédéric Mistral. Women's costumes traditionally consisted of full-skirted, long-sleeved dresses with fitted bodices and lace cuffs. The necklines of their bodices were decorated with shawl-like large collars, in muslin or lace, which came down to a point at the back, just above the waist. In front, they were draped and overlapped, forming a 'V' neck, and tucked into the belt. The hair was worn in a central parting, being drawn back softly, and curled up in a bun, covered with white lace, and encircled with a stiffened ribbon with projecting ends.

Men's costumes varied according to their occupations. Their 'best' clothes consisted of matching velvet jackets and waistcoats, worn with long trousers and felt hats or berets. The shepherds wore blue or grey smocks, sheepskin-trimmed cloaks, leggings, hob-nailed boots and berets.

Early morning between Vignon and Valensole

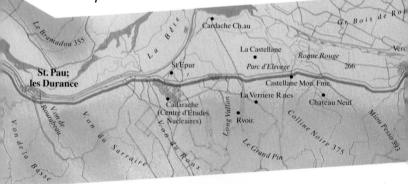

The market place at Vignon-sur-Verdon

The drove road on a plateau at St-Grégoire

Les Gorges du Verdon

At Vignon-sur-Verdon you can make a detour into
one of the most spectacular landscapes in France: les
Gorges du Verdon. In scenes reminiscent of Colorado's
Grand Canyon, the River Verdon has cut its way for
21km (13 miles) through the soft Jurassic limestone to
create a series of wild, deep and narrow gorges. In
some places the swift river runs 700m (2300 feet)
below the level of the surrounding plateau. The gorges
are of the greatest botanical and geological interest.

The best centre for an exploration is Castellane, to
the east of Vinon along the Route Lavande. Although
a road encircles the gorge and allows spectacular
views down into its depths from several lookouts, the
ideal way to see the canyons is on foot. The walk
through the main gorge takes about eight hours, with
the path passing through several tunnels. To go there
and back on opposite banks would take two days.
Guides advise walkers to stick to the marked path
because the level of the Verdon can rise rapidly.

23

A wine shop at Petit Logisson

The Medieval Town of Valensole and St Mayeul

The present site of Valensole was established by the Variacens tribe after the Romans withdrew their protection; the tribe had occupied a less defensible position at nearby Arlane. By the tenth century an important little city grew up, from which came St Mayeul (906–994), a son of the lord of the manor, who rose to become a national figure as abbot of the influential monastery at Cluny. The nineteenth-century architect Eugène Viollet-le-Duc called this abbey in Saône-et-Loire 'the mother of western civilization'. Six of its abbots were canonized. When St Mayeul died his property at Valensole passed to the monks of Cluny.

Crowning the rounded hill is the Gothic church of St Blaise and clustering around it are the streets of the old town. Remains of the medieval walls can be seen, including the twelfth-century Porte d'Aiguière. There are many beautiful eighteenth- and nineteenth-century houses in the old quarter.

Lavender cultivation: the area is called la Lavendoise

Vincent Van Gogh's Studio

The impressionist painter Vincent Van Gogh (1853–90) used a studio which stands on our route 10km (6 miles) beyond Valensole, overlooking the valley of the Asse from the top of a steep scarp. It was once a Musée Gogois, and some splashy murals remain. In between bouts of insanity Van Gogh painted ceaselessly in Arles. He committed suicide in July 1890.

Vincent Van Gogh's former studio

A roofscape at Valensole

Valensole and Admiral Villeneuve

Valensole was the birthplace of Vice-Admiral Pierre de Villeneuve (1763–1806), who commanded the allied French and Spanish fleets at the Battle of Trafalgar on 21st October 1805. The allied fleets had been blockaded in the Spanish port of Cadiz by a British fleet under Vice-Admiral Lord Nelson. Villeneuve, already in the bad books of his master, Napoleon I, heard that he was to be superseded in the command and decided to break out of Cadiz. In five hours the battle was over and Villeneuve, with his flagship *Bucentaure* dismasted, surrendered. He was imprisoned in England until the following April. Returning to France, he learnt that Napoleon was unforgiving and stabbed himself to death.

The family house where Villeneuve was brought up can be seen in Valensole. The village of Villeneuve itself lies some 10km (6 miles) to the north-west.

The Shepherds' Weekly Shopping Trip

In the days before shepherds had motor-cars, keeping the summer cabin stocked with provisions needed regular trips to the nearest village. On a fixed day of the week, say a Tuesday, the shepherds in the area would come down from the mountains, leaving their flocks to graze alone and hopefully out of harm's way. If two or three shepherds were sharing the same summer cabin, they might depute one of their number to run all their errands in town.

With each shepherd would come one or more donkeys, with pack saddles ready to carry back a week's stock of bread, vegetables and fruit for the people, salt for the sheep, maize flour for the dogs and any necessary medicines. The shepherds kept to a fixed day so that they could enjoy a fraternal gathering, which must have been something to look forward to after a solitary week in the mountains. Over a meal they exchanged not just gossip but also any novels they had finished reading. Then a final call was paid to the post office to pick up letters, newspapers and magazines before climbing back up the mountain.

A view of the River Asse from the drove road

Climbing with the railway towards Col du Labouret

Estoublon

Estoublon is a small village with ancient houses packed tightly in narrow streets. The place is dominated by the eighteenth-century Tour de l'Horloge, a pretty belltower which is a listed historic monument. After Estoublon the landscape becomes more spectacular and the drove road really seems to be entering the Alps proper.

The colourful scene on Digne's market day

Victorian Digne

Augustus Hare visited Digne towards the end of the last century and wrote the following description, which comes from his *South-Eastern France* (London, 1890):

> *Digne*, the Roman *Dinia*, the capital of the department of Basses-Alpes. The town, situated in a niche, by the usually dry bed of the Bléone, is divided into three parts – *la tête, le mitau (milieu), et le pied*. The principal promenade (Pré du Foire) near Hôtel Boyer, is rather picturesque, planted with plane-trees, and adorned with a statue (by Ramus of Marseilles) of Gassendi, the astronomer and demi-sceptic philosopher, born at Champtercier, near this, in 1592.
>
> Behind rises the tower of the cathedral [St Jérôme], crowned with open ironwork. The building has been so often

An Alpine peasant carrying hay (1900)

restored as to have little interest; the façade has a rose-window and a gothic portal with Christ and the symbolical beasts of the Apocalypse on the tympanum. In a chapel right of the nave is the tomb of a bishop, of 1615. A statue of S. Vincent de Paul is by Dalmas, 1869. A prison occupies the site of the episcopal palace.

Beyond the avenue of planes which opens from the Pré du Foire, at the end of the town, is the earlier cathedral of *Notre Dame* [du Bourg], of the twelfth and thirteenth centuries. Over the portal is a splendid rose-window, and the lions of the porch remain. The grandiose semi-desecrated interior is very striking and simple. It contains some remains of frescoes, and a number of mummified bodies are preserved in one of the transepts.

Shops in the old town at Digne

A fountain for thirsty sheep at La Javie

Today the town is better known as the *Capitale de la lavande* because of the widespread cultivation of lavender in the surrounding hills. There is a lavender fair in Digne each year at the end of August and the beginning of September.

The scientific interest of these Alpine foothills has been recognized by the creation nearby of the Alpes-de-Haute-Provence Geological Reserve.

There is a large and colourful market in Digne every Wednesday and Saturday. The town has spa facilities for rheumatism and respiratory conditions and there is a local museum in the old hospice.

The Sun King's Fortress at Seynes-les-Alpes

For centuries the Ubaye valley was in the front line of the struggle between Provence and then France against the Duchy of Savoy. In 1689 the French monarch Louis XIV – nicknamed the 'Sun King' because he once danced that role in a court ballet – stationed extra troops on the frontier with Piedmont, then part of Savoy, to persuade the fickle Duke Vittorio Amedeo of Savoy to remain his ally. The tactic failed and the following year the Savoyards nearly occupied Seynes, so Louis commissioned the military engineer Sébastien Vauban (1633–1707) to fortify its twelfth-century castle. Around the medieval keep Vauban built a modern cannonproof fortress whose bold bastions, though ruined, are still the most impressive structure in the town.

Between Seynes and the next fortress at St Vincent the drove road passes the Lac de Serre-Ponçon. One of the largest artificial lakes in Europe, it was formed in 1960 by damming the River Durance just below its confluence with the River Ubaye to supply hydro-electric power and water for irrigation.

Butterfly and thistle at Le Vernet

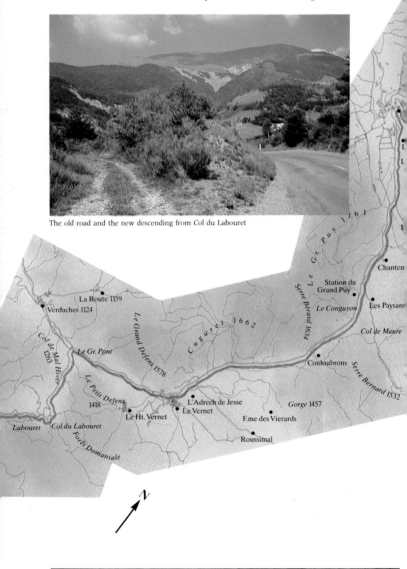
The old road and the new descending from Col du Labouret

Lac de Serre Ponçon, an artifical reservoir

A glimpse of the Alps from Le Martinet

St-Vincent-les-Forts and Piedmont

While Seynes was merely threatened in 1690, St Vincent was actually occupied by Piedmontese troops. Its strategic location at the junction of important roads in the Ubaye and Durance valleys, as well as its position on the frontier with Savoy, explains the proliferation of forts and gun batteries which surround it. There is a tour around them on a marked footpath.

The main fortress dates from 1691 and completely dominates the village: it is the work of Sébastien Vauban, like that at Seynes. The French philosopher Voltaire commented drily that Vauban constructed or repaired more than 150 fortifications and directed operations at 53 seiges in his efforts to extend the Sun King's empire.

Top of Col de Fours

Barcellonette and the Mexican Connection

Barcellonette is, among other things, the centre for the shepherds tending their flocks in the summer pastures which surround the upper valley of the Ubaye. The town enjoys a wide, flat site. It was founded in 1231 by permission of Raymond Bérengar IV, the Count of Provence. This noble Spanish family (known as Berenguer in Spain) also founded Barcelonette's better-known namesake, Barcelona, in Catalonia. The Provençal town was called Barcelone until the 1700s.

Because it is sited in the disputed frontier zone between Provence and Savoy, little has survived from the Middle Ages except some remnants of the fourteenth-century town walls and, overlooking the main square, the fifteenth-century Tour Cardinalis. This belfry of a Dominican convent is said to stand on the site of a Roman tower, although the nearest known Roman road of any consequence ran from Gap via the Durance valley to Briançon. In its well-ordered streets, now pedestrianized, the town retains the plan

A shepherd minding his flock at Le Super Sauze in July

of a former stronghold. Barcellonette became part of France in 1713.

During a rural depression in the nineteenth century many intrepid Barcellonais emigrated to Mexico. Such was their business acumen and knowledge of wool that they came more or less to monopolize the Mexican textile trade. Several returned with substantial fortunes to their native town and built splendid houses, quite foreign to such a remote valley. This accounts for the prosperous air of several boulevards

A bourgeois gateway in Victorian Barcellonette

The Barcellonais remember their
Mexican emigrants

outside the old town, lined with detached mansions
tricked out in the latest turn-of-the-century fashion
from Paris. The people here are well aware of this
inheritance, for not only has a book on the Mexican
connection been published locally, but a travel agent
does brisk business organizing trips to see the
remaining evidence of the emigration in Mexico.

Winter or summer, Barcellonette is a lovely little
town for a stay in the mountains. For once the visitors
actually seem to contribute to the charm of the place,
instead of spoiling its local character. A tradition of the
Ubaye valley which you may notice is the painting of
sundials on the southern face of old houses. At the
hamlet of Ferme de Rente on the drove road above
Barcellonette an example can be seen on an inn,
inscribed '1609 FUGIT TEMPUS/GAVOT L'ES PAS QU
VOUO'.

Nature in the Summer Pastures

Alpine pastures are famous for the enormous variety and abundance of their wild flowers. Why should this be? The explanation lies in the short growing season, sometimes less than three months in a year, which encourages rapid growth and development. The result is that species which flower in different months in more temperate climates all come into bloom together in the Alps. The monks who lived in the hospice at the summit of the Great St Bernard pass used to exploit their privileged location to cull the fragrant herbs and supply many a far-flung monastic pharmacy.

Among the commonest flowers are red rhododendrons, royal blue gentians and saxifrage. The diversity of species reaches a maximum at about 1500m (4900 feet) above sea-level, but above this height the number of different habitats decreases. Consequently in the uppermost zone above 4000m (13,000 feet) – that enjoyed by the edelweiss – only about ten species can

Lucky sheep enjoying the luscious grass of Champs des Fourches

From the stele at Las Cougnas

survive the peculiar conditions: in the clear air the sun can produce a temperature difference of 20 C (36 F) between opposite faces of a rock. The most abundant trees are all conifers: the silver fir, *Abies alba*, the Norway spruce, *Picea excelsa* and the larch, *Larix decidua*.

The chamois is the most sure-footed of Alpine creatures, but not often seen. It is discussed on page 130. The huge black Alpine crow is fairly common, if patchy in its distribution; but the Alpine eagle is very rare, perhaps now almost extinct. The sportsman Baillie Grohman described in his *Tyrol and the Tyrolese* a perilous adventure of the 1870s to snatch two young eagles from their inaccessible eyrie. Although admitting that there were thought to be only ten pairs left in Tyrol at the time, he spares not a thought for the effect his antics were having on the population.

Without the eagle the marmot, most charming of Alpine creatures, has no natural predator. This shy little mammal, looking like a tiny fat beaver, lives above the tree line where it likes to be able to see for miles across its kingdom. Marmots are not readily visible but you will hear their shrill penetrating whistles as they warn each other of your approach.

St-Etienne-de-Tinée

The top of Vallon de la Moutière

THE WALDENSIANS' GLORIOUS RETURN

Lux Lucet in Tenebris

This, perhaps our most romantic route, will take you in the footsteps of a band of men, fiercely determined to return to their homeland from exile in order to fight for their religious beliefs, the Waldensians, a Protestant sect which survives to this day on the Franco-Italian border and in the United States and South America.

The origin of the Waldensian sect is usually traced back to Valdes, later known as Peter Waldo; his followers are variously known as Waldensians, Vaudois or Valdesi. Valdes was a rich merchant in Lyons, in south-eastern France. About 1170, awoken to a deeper sense of reality by the sudden death of a friend, he sold all his goods to feed the poor and started a brotherhood of poor men. He had the Bible translated into Provençal, and he and companions, taking the triple vow of chastity, poverty and obedience, wandered about preaching.

In his approach to religion and the world Valdes was close to his near contemporary Francis of Assisi, but while Francis was taken up and sanctified by the Church a very different fate was in store for Valdes and his disciples. Pope Alexander III sanctioned their vows, but forbade them to preach without permission from the local Church authority, the Archbishop of Lyons. When they refused to accept this condition the Archbishop denounced them as heretics and expelled them from his diocese. The movement spread, but many were tried and condemned for heresy, then burned alive.

The surviving Waldensians gradually took refuge in remote and sparsely populated valleys in Piedmont. There they stayed throughout the Middle Ages, keeping themselves separate from the Roman Church, and from time to time enjoying the protection of their rulers, the Counts (later Dukes) of Savoy, in exchange for the payment of taxes.

The Waldensians sometimes accepted the ministrations of the Church's priests during their early years in the valleys, but the distinctive mark of their teaching was the study of the Bible. Until 1550 they had no churches of their own, holding their assemblies in the fields or in caves.

When news of Martin Luther's defiance of papal authority – the start of the Reformation – reached the valleys, Protestant reformers from

Switzerland were invited to come to state their case to a Waldensian synod in 1532. By accepting the articles of faith proposed by the Swiss the Waldensians merged with the Swiss Calvinist movement. In later centuries they were regarded as having been Protestants before the Reformation.

Waldensian costume painted from life by Estella Canziani in about 1910

The first persecution of the Waldensians came in 1560–61 when France, Spain and Savoy signed a secret treaty to exterminate heresy vigorously. Nearly one hundred years later another fierce persecution began when 700 of the Duke of Savoy's troops invaded Val Pellice. In 1655 a terrible massacre known as the Piedmontese Easter raged throughout the valley. It aroused horror among Protestants as far away as England, where the Puritan poet John Milton wrote his sonnet 'On the Late Massacher in *Piemont*' (page 45). The atrocity led the Lord Protector of England, Oliver Cromwell, to send an ambassador to Turin to complain. The Duke of Savoy is said to have yielded to the eloquence of the envoy's Latin oration and agreed to an amnesty.

In 1685 the Sun King Louis XIV, then at the zenith of his imperial power, outlawed Protestantism in France by revoking the tolerant Edict of Nantes. At this time the Waldensians' valleys were surrounded on both their west and north-east sides by French territory. The following January Louis's nephew, Duke Vittorio Amedeo II of Savoy, yielded to pressure and issued a similar decree. Prospects for the Waldensians began to look grim indeed.

Swiss delegates who had been to Turin and tried unsuccessfully to intercede for their fellow Calvinists now attempted to persuade the Waldensians that exile from their valleys was the only solution. But through the influence of Henri Arnaud, a militant French pastor from Dauphiné, the Waldensians decided to stand and resist, relying on Divine protection. A devastating pincer movement by the combined French and Savoyard armies overcame this resistance, and more than 10,000 of the 14,000 inhabitants of the valleys were either killed or taken prisoner.

Some of the captives died, others were sold into slavery on Venetian galleys or were converted to Catholicism. The remainder, after months of terrible incarceration in fortresses in Piedmont, were escorted into exile by Swiss and Savoyard guards. After crossing Mont Cenis pass in the January of 1687 just 2490 Waldensians received a welcome as Protestant martyrs from the good people of Geneva.

At this point the famous episode of the Glorious Return begins. Some of the survivors scattered to try to find homes in other parts of Switzerland and southern Germany, but the more zealous Waldensians resisted attempts to move them from their refugee camps. Henri

The Waldensian coat of arms with their motto meaning 'The light shineth in the darkness'

Arnaud now proved himself to be a spiritually minded man with a gift for military leadership and persuasive oratory. He urged his comrades to return to their homeland and fight.

Meanwhile William of Orange was forming an alliance of Protestant states against Louis XIV. He appreciated that Vittorio Amedeo's fidelity to Louis was in considerable doubt, and that the Waldensians were in a position to conduct guerrilla operations against the French army which had been stationed on the Savoy frontier. With encouragement from William, Arnaud secretly formed a corps of some 900 men, 500 of them Waldensians, in the forests around Lac Léman (Lake Geneva) during August 1689.

While the result of all this political manoeuvring was the resettlement of the valleys in Piedmont, it is important to realize that the Glorious Return was actually a commando raid, led in the name of Christ by fanatical Protestants during a war of religion that was also a power struggle. Although the Waldensians were inspired by the hope of recapturing the valleys where their people had lived for five centuries, the expedition itself consisted of able-bodied if untrained soldiers without their families.

For fourteen days the little army marched from the south bank of Lac Léman around the flank of Mont Blanc, across the Col d'Iseran and over the long pass of Mont Cenis to reach Bobbio Pellice. Several skirmishes with the French forces left Arnaud with only 300 men, whom he led in a desperate battle the following spring at the village of Balziglia. The battered Waldensians were saved when the ever-fickle Vittorio Amedeo broke his treaty with Louis, joined the Protestant Grand Alliance and allowed the refugees to return from Germany and Switzerland to rebuild their communities in the valleys.

The triumph had one ironic footnote: it became a condition of the 1697 Treaty of Ryswick which ended the war that all Frenchmen were to be expelled from the valleys. So Arnaud, as a French subject born in Dauphiné, died in exile from the valleys of Piedmont which he had adopted and helped to save.

What of the pathway itself? Fortunately we can trace the Waldensians' steps almost exactly because their leader wrote a detailed account soon after the event.

Arnaud relates that it took the band just ten days to reach their northernmost valley, Val Germanasca, and a further four days of manoeuvring to reach their main base, Val Pellice. Although many of them would have been able to find their own way from previous experience during fine weather, the soldiers found it prudent to adopt a policy of taking hostages to act as guides, and the richer the better. The value of a hostage for bargaining was likely to decrease once he was out of the area where he was known, for the preferred tactic was to negotiate a passage through a town or over a bridge without resorting to force.

During the first two days the going was comparatively easy. The soldiers negotiated their way successfully through Yvoire, Boëge, Cluses and Sallanches. After Megève on the third day, however, they faced the first physical barrier in the shape of a vertical wall of rock called Aiguille Croche. To cross this sharp ridge they had to detour to the west over the Croix de Pierre in steady rain. Then they had to negotiate a series of remote passes, La Fenêtre, La Bonhomme and Croix de Bonhomme, around the western flank of Mont Blanc.

The tricky burghers of Ste-Foy-Tarentaise tried to lure the Waldensians into accepting copious hospitality – a device to delay them until the arrival of the Savoyard militia. The villages in these Alpine valleys had nearly all been abandoned at the news of the Waldensians' approach: there was often no one to pay for the provisions they found in deserted barns.

More serious mountaineering was in store at the Col d'Iseran (2770m; 9088 feet) and then the long Mont Cenis pass where they lost their way: some became separated and never rejoined the group, while others were obliged to slide down a steep slope on their bottoms.

On the banks of the Dora Riparia their luck in avoiding the enemy came to an end. A Savoyard scouting force followed the Waldensians up the valley to the strategic bridge at Salbertrand, where 2500 French troops were waiting for them. Against all odds the Waldensians carried this bridge and struggled on through the night to reach Val Germanasca at first light.

Now the survivors split up into several companies of guerrillas, and a more brutal phase of warfare began. Forty-six Savoyard soldiers in pursuit across the Col du Pis from Salbertrand were captured and put to death on the bridge at Balziglia. The tactics were cruel, but the Waldensians were fighting for possession of the most beautifully rich valleys. In the final stretch of the walk you enter Val Pellice at a natural Garden of Eden, the hamlet of Podio, perched in a spectacular position among orchards and pastures at the head of the valley.

And a walk it really is: no one but a madman would try to follow the Waldensians on a bicycle across the Croix de Pierre, around Mont Blanc and over the Mont Cenis pass.

Today the Waldensians remain the most important indigenous community of Protestants in Italy. The spiritual solidarity which has been such a feature of their history reveals itself in the social services which they perform without reference to the Italian State. And a weary traveller who has followed our route to the end will be sure to find a warm welcome at the nearby *Foresteria Valdese*, the Waldensians' hostel for foreigners.

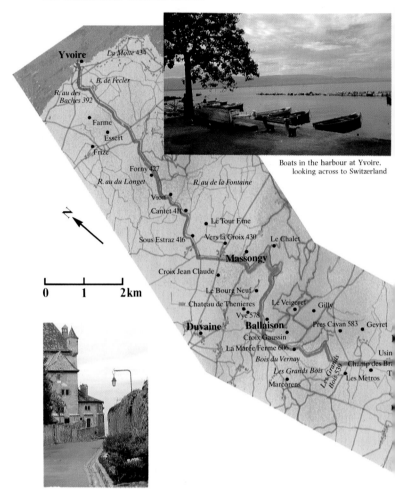

Boats in the harbour at Yvoire,
looking across to Switzerland

The walls of medieval Yvoire

Medieval Yvoire: Start of the Glorious Return

Yvoire is a well-preserved medieval town occupying a strategic position on the Savoyard bank of Lac Léman. It is the most important surviving example of fourteenth-century military architecture in the region. Its castle dominates the lakeside, and also guards the gates leading west to Geneva and east to Thonon. A substantial fragment of the town walls still stands. Duke Amedeo V of Savoy ordered these fortifications to be built in 1306, and the work was complete in ten years.

The pretty fishing harbour and the agreeably random arrangement of the old houses and their tiled roofs attract numerous visitors to Yvoire. Local historians are aware of Arnaud's exploits here, but call the Waldensians *Luzernois*: an old name for their main valley in Piedmont is Luzerna.

In his account of the Glorious Return Henri Arnaud records that after landing just west of the town:

> Some officers and twelve privates were sent
> to Ivoire, to persuade the inhabitants to lay
> down their arms and grant a passage. The
> inhabitants, understanding that a refusal
> would expose them to the perils of the sword
> and fire, granted all that was required of
> them; but did not the less omit to light up
> their beacon, which might have entailed on
> them the performance of the threat, had not

the Vaudois been in a disposition to admit the profferred excuse, 'that some children had done it in mistake.' As a condition, however, of pardon for this offence, the castellain and salt exciseman were required to perform the office of guides.

By Night across the Lake

During the Waldensians' brief exile in Switzerland, the ardent Arnaud took every opportunity to instil a martial spirit in his comrades. Persuaded by his imaginative and fiery rhetoric, 800 adventurers assembled from Germany and Switzerland, meeting secretly by night in forests between Nion and Rolle on the Swiss shore of Lac Léman.

By the night of 16 August 1689 Arnaud was ready to move. Seizing a flotilla of boats at Prangins, he and his men crossed to Savoy at a point where the lake is only three or four kilometres wide. The Waldensians landed on the southern bank near the little port of Yvoire. Outside the village some temporary earthworks thrown up by the little army can still be seen.

War memorial at Boege

The Chablais countryside and Lac Léman (Lake Geneva)

The First Day's March to Cormand

Arnaud's own account continues, describing the tactics for passing potentially hostile towns:

> As night came on, they stopped near Viu [Viuz-en-Sallaz] and released one of the gentlemen [a hostage] who could not well support the fatigue of walking. After they had halted long enough to give time to the inhabitants to disperse, in case they had assembled under arms, they entered at twilight; and, having obtained refreshments for money, departed again two hours after the moon had risen. After an hour's march they were overtaken by the night, and the hostages were desired to write another note to the town of St Joyre [St Jeoire], through which they had to pass. On their arrival at this place, instead of opposition, they met with a most friendly reception from the inhabitants, who crowded to see them; and the magistrates even ordered a cask of wine into the middle of the street to be used by the soldiers at their discretion. . . . Leaving this place, they crossed some shelving

[Map with place names: Les Crets, Le Foron, La Lechere 708, Thezier, Burguigny, Pont Beguin, Vinz en Sallaz, Le Faubourg, Bregny, Ch.au au Gaillard, La Tour 632, Chez Gavillet, Le Brochet 606, Les Tattes, La Tour d'en Bas, Les Moulins, Puilly, La Pavoire, Bois de Chaffard, Bois de l'Herbette, Ch.au de Beauregard, Previères, Chez Catrioux, Entreverges, Chez Mille, Marais d'Entreverges, St Jeoire, Montrena 564, Les Epetires, Bois de Viuz, Reservoir 619, Le Risse 523, Clos Ruffy, Chez les Jacquard, La Palud, Sur Cocu, Cormand, Pont du Risse, Pont du Giffre, Les Combes, Le Plan Seraphin 498, Cormand et Devaut, Le Pery Ferme, La Con, Ossat. Compass showing N pointing down-left.]

ground till they came to a little hill, where they halted in an open plain called Carman [Cormand]. It was midnight, and rainy; yet it was resolved to wait for day-break, in order that their strength might be recruited by a little rest and sleep, before they crossed the river at Marni [Marignier]. . . .

A wooden house at Cormand

Fretted balconies at Cormand, where the Waldensians stopped

On the 16th of August, about ten in the morning, they approached Cluses, through which it was absolutely necessary to pass. The inhabitants, however, had armed and lined the trenches; while the peasants, who had descended from the mountains, loaded the Vaudois with abuse; who, advancing within musket-shot under an incessant rain, determined to force the passage. . . . The inhabitants now saw that the affair was serious, and without further hesitation granted the passage.

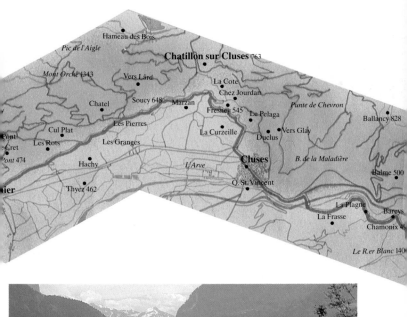

A distant view of Cluses, where a passage was negotiated

Savoyard house near Hauteluce

The Second Day's March to Combloux

Leaving Cluses the Waldensians found an agent in their midst bearing a message to Sallanches. Arnaud wrote:

> In these letters was an exhortation to arms, and a direction to attack the Vaudois in front, while the people of Cluses would do so on the rear. Expecting opposition, and resolved on defence, the Vaudois defiled along a very narrow valley, hemmed in by lofty mountains, where a whole army might be stopped with stones; and this the more easily at that time, when the Arve, swollen by frequent rains, left scarcely room enough for the road.

The peasants, though under arms, stood by to watch them pass, but the band found the passage of Sallanches a much greater obstacle. At first the castellan and three syndics tried to delay them while a defence force assembled. Then four Capuchin friars

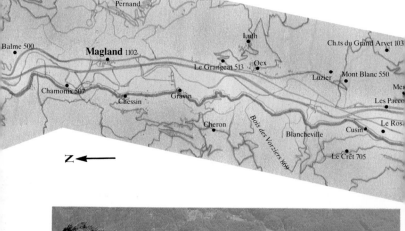

The cosmopolitan promenade in Sallanches

interceded and tricked them into exchanging two distinguished and useful hostages for the miller and a 'pitiable wretch'.

> Indignant at this shameful fraud, Monsieur Arnaud advanced with the intention of detaining the Capuchins. His countenance seemed to betray his intention; for so cleverly did the good friars tuck up their gowns for a race, that only two were secured.

The Waldensians now advanced seriously in line of battle, but the 600 armed inhabitants held their fire, fearing that their town might be burnt.

> Our people thus advanced quietly, and, after a tortuous route, arrived at the village of Cablau [Combloux]. There the repose so necessary after a long march over bad roads and in incessant rain, was but incomplete; for neither could they procure provisions to allay hunger, nor fire by which they might dry themselves.

Church spire at Hauteluce

Mont Blanc from Megève

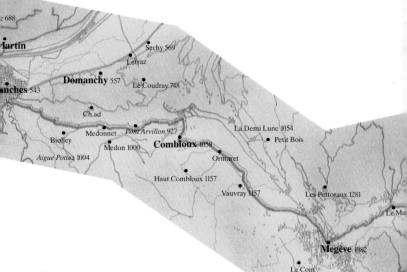

Puritan Support

When news of the slaughter in the valleys of Piedmont reached England John Milton wrote one of his most powerful sonnets, 'On the Late Massacre in *Piemont*':

Avenge O Lord thy slaughter'd Saints, whose bones
   Lie scatter'd on the Alpine mountains cold,
   Ev'n them who kept thy truth so pure of old
   When all our Fathers worship't Stocks and Stones,
Forget not: in thy book record their groanes
   Who were thy Sheep and in thy antient Fold
   Slayn by the bloody *Piemontese* that roll'd
   Mother with Infant down the Rocks. Their moans
The Vales redoubl'd to the Hills, and they
   To Heav'n. Their martyr'd blood and ashes sow
   O're all th'*Italian* fields where still doth sway
The triple Tyrant: that from these may grow
   A hunder'd-fold, who having learnt thy way
   Early may fly the *Babylonian* wo.

A fresco at Belleville

The March across Mont Blanc

On their third day, the 19th of August 1689, the Waldensians faced the climb across the western flank of Mont Blanc itself. In the words of their pastor Arnaud:

> If the Vaudois were no longer disturbed by the motions of the people of Cluses, Maglan, and Salenche, they were not a little alarmed when they learned the difficult nature of the day's journey before them, for they had to cross two of the rudest mountains of Savoy.

La Balme, where the Waldensians stayed under dreadful conditions

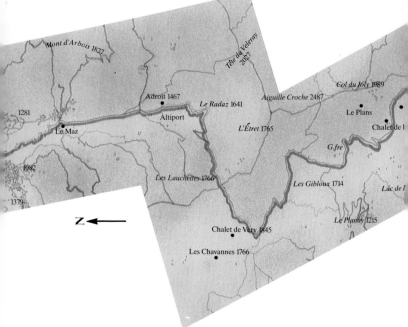

Arnaud meant the Aiguille Croche and Aiguille de Roselette. Both seem formidable rocky barriers as you approach from this side: the former cliff towers 1000m (3300 feet) above, seeming to close the valley as you pass the little Megève airstrip. The only way to cross is to veer right (west) over a subsidiary ridge at Pré Rosset, from where you can see that a good footpath leads diagonally up the grassy slope to the main crest at Croix de Pierre. This lives up to its name because the point where you are to cross the ridge is marked by a silhouetted cross. The second crest, Aiguille de Roselette, is then crossed by Col de la Fenêtre.

Arnaud's band slid down from this pass late at night, and he wrote:

> On this spot, deep as an abyss, desert and
> cold, the Vaudois were compelled to halt,
> with no fuel but what they obtained by
> unroofing the huts which sheltered them
> from the rain, thus escaping one misery at
> the expense of encountering another.

Crête des Gittes

But nowadays you find civilization in this remote valley in the form of the Refuge de la Balme at a height of 1706m (5597 feet). It is also easier to find your way from here, because at la Balme you join two well used footpaths, the Grande Randonnée 5 and the Tour de Mont Blanc. On their fourth day the Waldensians marched over the two Bonhomme passes knee-deep in snow – in Arnaud's words:

> . . . in continual expectation of a bloody
> action, for they knew that, during the
> preceding year, good forts, intrenchments
> with embrasures and counterscarps, had

been made in this quarter. . . . But the Eternal, who was ever present with this troop of the faithful, permitted them to find these fine fortifications unguarded; the troops having long evacuated them in weariness of so long and useless occupation. . . .

A view of the Croix de Pierre (on the ridge to the right) near Megève

Waldensian soldiers from
Arnaud's band

Sweet Words at Ste-Foy-Tarentaise

During the fifth day of their march the Waldensians reached the village of Ste-Foy-Tarentaise, dominating the gorge of the River Isère. Having started from Séez before dawn, they called a rest halt outside the village. Arnaud records:

> they were astonished at the obliging reception they met with. Many gentlemen, and a large portion of the peasantry, came out to meet them, and addressed them with great civility, expressing joy at seeing them, and praise of their purpose to return to their own country. They even pressed us to pass the night among them, and said they would bake bread, slay cattle, and give wine to refresh the soldiers.

After five days of marching, often through rain and with hardly any sleep, these honeyed words had an alluring effect on some of the Waldensians. However, Arnaud, ever distrustful of the apparent kindness of an enemy, recognized in these offers from Ste-Foy another delaying tactic. He successfully persuaded his officers that to stay might allow Savoyard troops to find them.

The Torrent des Glaciers flanking Mont Blanc

So the Waldensians moved on and, for good measure, Arnaud took hostage those flattering gentlemen who had made the enticing invitation.

As we approach the headwaters of the Isère the valley becomes tighter and tighter. The Waldensians had to cross the tortuous stream repeatedly on simple Alpine bridges of beams suspended over the torrent. They were lucky in that, although the inhabitants of the settlements had fled, they had not thrown down the bridges. The armed peasants could be seen on the heights, but did not disturb the intruders, who could therefore enjoy the luxury of camping in a meadow around a large fire.

Lettering from a Waldensian manuscript

Scree slopes in Val d'Isère

The Sixth Day's March over Col d'Iseran

On the 22nd of August, the sixth day of their journey, the Waldensians began by marching a short distance into the little town of Tignes. There they demanded the return of some money which appears to have been taken from two Waldensian scouts. 'The inhabitants,' remarks Arnaud, 'were, indeed, well pleased to escape on making this simple restitution; for they had expected exemplary punishment.' Arnaud also rotated his hostages; those remaining were released, and the soldiers 'invited' two local priests and an advocate to replace them.

Tignes is almost the only place where you cannot follow directly in the footsteps of the Waldensians, for there in 1953 the French completed the highest dam in Europe, 180m (590 feet) from top to bottom including the foundations. The reservoir flooded the old site, and the village was rebuilt as Tignes-les-Boisses just west of the dam.

About 6km (4 miles) up the valley, at the famous ski resort of Val d'Isère, our path branches right off the D902 road and follows the Grande Randonnée 5 long-distance footpath for about 9km (6 miles) over the Col d'Iseran. The D902 also crosses this pass at a height of 2770m (9088 feet) above sea-level – the highest pass road in Europe – and rejoins the footpath in Val d'Arc.

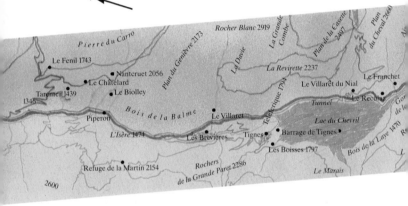

Looking towards Col d'Iseran, the highest pass road in Europe

The Waldensians Receive a Warning

Arnaud told how the Waldensians crossed the pass:

> They began to ascend the mountain of La
> Maurienne, sometimes called Tisserans,
> instead of Mont Iseran. . . . Some very
> painful ground was traversed among Alps,
> where there was a great abundance of
> cattle. The shepherds, instead of running
> away, regaled our travellers; and gave them
> to understand that they would have great
> difficulty in returning to their own country;
> for though their march had not yet been
> opposed, it would be so, strenuously, at the
> foot of Mont Cenis, by a considerable force,
> who were there firmly awaiting them.

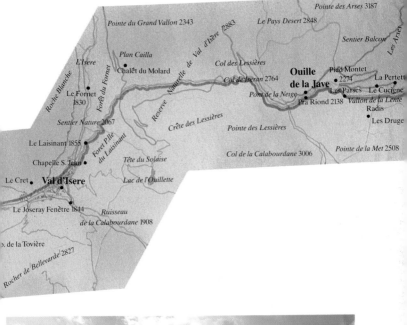

Vanoise on the way to Col d'Iserar

The Battle for the Bridge at Salbertrand

It is a testimony to the mountain-craft of the Waldensians during the Glorious Return that in the main they managed to avoid both the French and Savoyard armies with only one exception. That was when they were obliged to descend from the heights in order to cross the River Dora at Salbertrand.

A path near Bessans tempts us into the Alps

Gentians in Vallon de Savine

To evade the garrison at Susa and the strong fort at Exilles in the middle of the Dora valley, Arnaud kept to the heights on the northern bank of the River Dora. But there they met a company of French infantry, whose captain lured the Waldensians into a trap. As Arnaud's men descended the valley to evade the French and cross by the bridge near Salbertrand, they found their passage disputed by the Marquis de Larrey and 2500 more French troops.

The Waldensians were hemmed in between the rocks and the river, with the pursuing infantry pressing their rear. The trapped men had no choice but to advance in the face of a fearful volley of two thousand shots. Because their retreat was completely cut off the Waldensians made a desperate charge across the bridge, and such was their impetuosity that the enemy was routed. Seeing this the Marquis de

Larrey cried out: 'Is it possible that I have lost the battle, and my own honour?' and fled over the Mont Genèvre pass to Briançon, and beyond. The Waldensians were able to proceed on their march unimpeded.

Unfortunately the historic bridge at Salbertrand no longer exists, for along the river run the tracks from the earliest railway tunnel under the Alps, the Fréjus, completed in 1871, and when it was constructed all the river bridges had to be raised to clear the railway as well. We have one consolation, though: the road to the modern bridge is called the Via Arnaud.

Chalets near Mont Cenis (1827)

The village of Le Collet, called La Madeleine by Arnaud

The path across Mont Cenis in Vallon de Savine

The Seventh Day's March over the Mont Cenis Pass

After crossing Col d'Iseran Arnaud's band marched down the River Arc as far as the village of Le Collet. Finding it deserted, they camped nearby without shelter in a drenching rain. The following morning, after exchanging hostages at Lanselevillard, they tackled the long Mont Cenis pass. Arnaud writes:

> Having gained the summit, and knowing there was a post-house near it which might forward a true account of their progress, they sent a party to seize on all the horses which they could find. The sufferings of the Vaudois in crossing the Great and Little Mont Cenis surpass imagination. . . . They unfortunately lost their way on the descent; an accident which might have originated either from the malice of their guides, the density of the fog, or from the new, and therefore trackless snow. In consequence of this error, their descent was over precipices rather than by a path.

The descent at Col Clapier is indeed extremely steep. The Mont Cenis was one of several well-used passes where carriages once had to be dismantled and carried over the mountain. The English traveller Thomas Watkin described the practice in the 1780s:

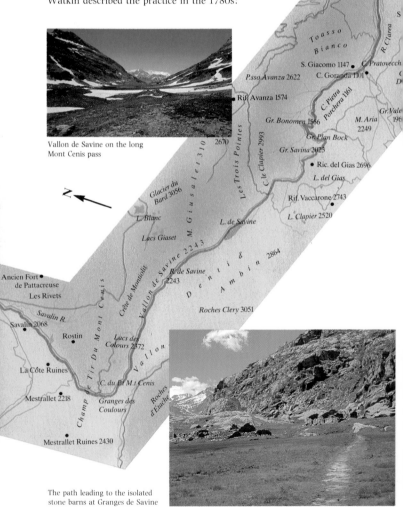

Vallon de Savine on the long
Mont Cenis pass

The path leading to the isolated
stone barns at Granges de Savine

Early next morning our guides took the carriage to pieces, which they put on the backs of some noble mules and slung the body between two of these animals. We each had a mule; but, having determined to walk all the way, left them to the postilion, and began our journey on foot. Travellers are frequently carried over by men in a chair, something similar to a sedan, but much lighter for such a journey.

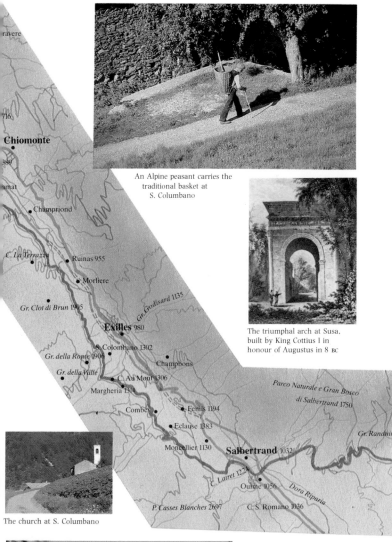

An Alpine peasant carries the traditional basket at S. Columbano

The triumphal arch at Susa, built by King Cottius I in honour of Augustus in 8 BC

The church at S. Columbano

Sunrise on Cima Vallonetto

The path above Joussaud

The Battle of Balziglia

In the months following their return to the valleys, Henri Arnaud's band pursued a guerrilla war against the French. The Waldensians played hit and run, wearing for identification orange ribbons that symbolized the House of Orange which led the anti-French coalition. They are said to have attacked on three successive days places as widely scattered as Prali, Perrero and Pomareto, so that the enemy never knew where to expect them next.

As winter drew closer the guerrillas provisioned a rocky fortress, mostly by capturing food and ammunition from the French. At Balziglia, at the head of a valley which leads into the Val Germanasca, stands a rampart of rock which blocks the defile and forms a secure natural defence. In caves hollowed in

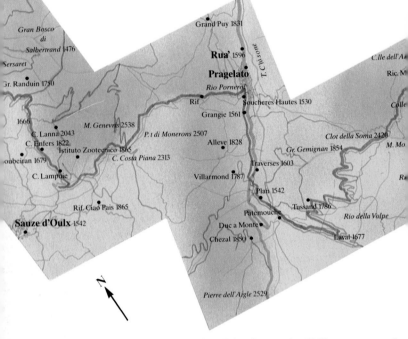

the sides of this fortress the Waldensians spent the winter waiting for an onslaught.

The next spring the French commander, Marshal Nicolas de Catinat, sent 4000 dragoons under the command of the Marquis de Feuquière to exterminate the Waldensians. The Marquis made numerous assaults on the rock without dislodging the little garrison, so that eventually he forced peasants to haul

Colle Costa Piana

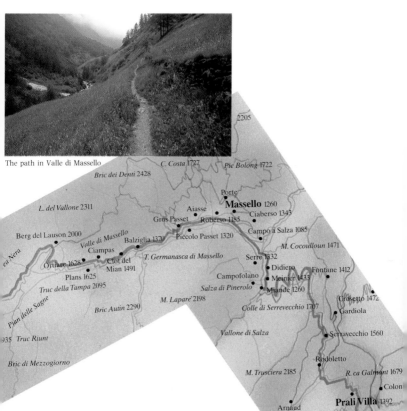

The path in Valle di Massello

cannon up the ravine. Driven from their positions by the ensuing bombardment, the defenders waited as they thought for death – to be saved by the providential descent of a thick fog, which prevented the French soldiers from seeing the Waldensians as they made their escape.

The guerrillas were able to crawl along a dangerous precipice undetected and so escape across the mountains, while the over-confident French commander sent word to Paris that the 'rebels' were captured. As it turned out a second deliverance for the Waldensians was at hand, for Louis xiv and the fickle Duke of Savoy had fallen out and the duke proclaimed a general amnesty. The persecution of the Waldensians was over, barring a further brief period in 1730.

Near Pian di Fea Nera

Balziglia, where the Waldensians fought a battle in 1690

General Beckwith: a One-legged Champion

Like the Jews and the Franciscans, the Waldensians survived the violence of the fourteenth century through sheer spiritual solidarity. Their persistence in dissent made them many Protestant friends, of whom one of the staunchest was the English soldier General Charles Beckwith (1789–1862).

Beckwith came from a military family. He was a veteran of the Peninsular War of 1808–14, and at the age of only twenty-six fought, as a brevet major, in the Battle of Waterloo which finally defeated Napoleon in 1815. He had the misfortune to lose his leg during the engagement but was promoted to lieutenant-colonel.

In the words of his nineteenth-century biographer H. M. Stephens, he 'hardly knew to what occupation a one-legged man could turn, when he happened one day in 1827, while waiting in the library of Apsley House [the Duke of Wellington's London mansion], to look into Dr Gilly's book on the Waldenses'.

His curiosity aroused, Beckwith paid a visit to Piedmont and discovered more of the Waldensians' past history. There he observed at first hand their poverty and ignorance – this was twenty years before the King of Savoy granted them the same civil rights as Catholics – and at once determined to play his part.

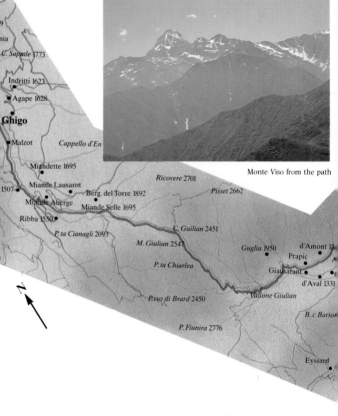

Monte Viso from the path

At last the man of action had found a vocation to suit his restless spirit: to educate the Waldensians and to reanimate their evangelical faith. For the last thirty-five years of his life he lived among them, founding no fewer than 120 village schools in their valleys. In his perpetual tours of inspection to check on progress, the eccentric and one-legged figure of the English soldier –

promoted to major-general in 1846 – inspired great respect and affection, so that when he died thousands of peasants flocked to his funeral.

Ask after him in any Waldensian village or hamlet you please and the people will show you the school he founded. It is a living testimony to the education system Beckwith started that your inquiry can be in rapid French or Italian, while the response may well come from a farmer with a university degree!

The statue of Henri Arnaud

The path in Vallone Giulian

Baussan

Airali 475

Luserna
Lusernetta

Torre Pellice 545

Coppieri 612

Castellazzo 1410

Chabriols 723

Rocca Berra 1231

La Portaccia 1482

Bonissa

Rocca Fautet 1695   Ciarmis 787

T. Pellice

Bodeina 902

Villar Pellice 666

Rua'

Garnier

a 1329

Buffa

Cognetti 701

io Pellice 734   Perla' 723

Alsas

ello 865

The Casa Valdese, 1889, the library and meeting room of the Waldensian synod at Torre Pellice

Podio, a 'Garden of Eden'

THE ITALIAN ALPS AND LAKES

Valleys of Isolation

This route is a west-to-east walk of some 470km (295 miles) along the length of the Italian Alps from near the French border almost to the Yugoslav frontier. We have chosen this route because it provides a fascinating ethnographical study: while to some extent all the people of the Alps share a common way of living, the difficulty of passing between valleys separated by rugged mountains has led to communities developing independently and preserving their individual cultures over the centuries.

The route highlights an astonishing range of cultures in the string of south-facing valleys along the longest border in the Alps. To describe

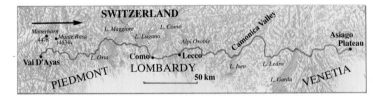

N

the route in the simplest terms, those of linguistics, it begins in French-speaking Val d'Aosta; moves through a Walser dialect of German that is native to Val Gressoney and Upper Valsesia; returns briefly to French in Lower Valsesia; passes through a long, Italian-speaking section in the lake districts of Milan, Bergamo, Brescia and Trent; to end in the so-called 'Sette Comuni' who speak the Cimbro language, incomprehensible to Germans and Italians alike.

Although language can and does evolve through immigration, or changes in the pattern of people's occupations, in these Alpine valleys the governing factor is the ease or difficulty of communication between one part and another. In Val d'Aosta, which has good links with France through both the Little and Great St Bernard passes, the French language has been kept up to date since the Middle Ages by a constant flow of travellers. The neighbouring Val Gressoney and Upper Valsesia are both dead-end valleys to all but determined foot-sloggers, and there the original German has become corrupted into a distinctive dialect.

But do not be alarmed into thinking that you will need to master all these arcane dialects in order to make yourself understood as you pass through the Italian Alps. For whichever tongue is native, every valley-dweller has been obliged, at least since the First World War, to learn Italian at school.

Even if you do not hear these languages spoken, let alone try to speak them yourself, you can appreciate the linguistic difference on signs in the streets and in the shops. You can study them in advance on a large-scale map, where the French, German and Italian place-names can easily be separated out. Readers who love poring over maps may like to know of some place-name endings left behind by former invaders and refugees, most of them many centuries ago. For example, *-asco* is Ligurian, *-enna* is Etruscan, *-iano* is Roman, and *-engo* is Lombardic. You can get some idea of the time scales involved if you remember that the Ligurians were the prehistoric settlers in the region, the Etruscans are believed to have come to Italy around 1000 BC, the Romans ruled the whole of Italy from the 200s BC to the AD 400s, and the Lombards were a Germanic people who ruled much of northern Italy from AD 568 to 774.

The north end of Lake Garda and the little port of Riva which were Austrian until the First World War

Most of the early settlement in northern Italy, from about 1500 BC, was around the lakes, each formed in a glacial valley dammed by a terminal moraine. There is a particularly good collection of Bronze Age material in the museum at Como, which lies at the base of a lake which formed part of a prehistoric route into the Alps. Excavations have uncovered the remains of Bronze Age dwellings built on wooden piles at the water's edge on Lakes Como, Maggiore, Garda, Idro and Ledro. A reconstruction can be seen in the museum on the banks of Lake Ledro. It is interesting to reflect that the use of wooden piles to provide the foundations for Venice is a direct descendant of the building methods of these Bronze Age people. You might like to turn to the Amber Route (pages 120–151) for a description of prehistoric trade through Alpine passes.

The Romans established a province covering the Italian Alps, known as *Gallia Cisalpina* (literally 'Gaul *this* side of the Alps'), in the first century BC. They finally conquered the Alps in about 17 BC under their first emperor, Augustus. To commemorate this achievement they built a vast monument at La Thurbie in a prominent position on the coast of Monaco, where Italia once met the new Roman province of Alpes Maritimae.

The Romans quickly established a co-ordinated military road network, and founded towns to guard the approaches to the main passes into the Alpine provinces. Augusta Praetoria (now Aosta) stood at the junction of the roads leading from the Little and Great St Bernard passes; Comum (Como) controlled the Splügen and Julier passes; Tridentum (Trent or Trento) guarded the easiest pass of all, the

Brenner; and Invillino (Santino near Tolmezzo) blocked the approach from the Plöcken Pass to the important Adriatic port of Aquileia.

The most dramatic remains of the Roman occupation of the Italian Alps are at Aosta and Como, which still preserve their Roman street plans almost intact. Our path affords a graphic view of the Como street plan as it climbs steeply to Brunate, while the museum in the town has a good collection of Roman remains.

Survivals from the Middle Ages are confined almost entirely to castles and churches. The castles in Val d'Aosta form a set which has survived almost intact despite being on a major invasion route into Piedmont. The most splendid of all is the Castle of Issogne near the mouth of Val d'Ayas, a late medieval residence rebuilt in 1497–98, when it was decorated with a remarkable series of frescos showing scenes from everyday life.

Most of the churches were rebuilt and refurnished during and after the Counter-Reformation of the 1500s. The proximity of Protestants, with their more austere ideas of religious buildings, led the artists who decorated these churches to adopt an extreme style of baroque. It would be easy to imagine yourself in Spain when you look at some of the church interiors of Lombardy.

Although the naves of these churches have been modified out of all recognition the builders often left the medieval bell-towers untouched, so the work of a famous school of Romanesque masons in Como can be seen in bell-towers along our route from Valganna, west of Lake Lugano, and also in fortifications.

Most of the surviving historic buildings and monuments are from the eighteenth and nineteenth centuries, and in them too regional variations are to be seen. For example, between Valsesia and Lake Maggiore there is a strong tradition of painting *trompe l'oeil* architectural details on the outside walls of churches and houses. Further east there is a sudden and striking change from tall German churches on the remote plateau of Asiago to refined Venetian temples in the style of the sixteenth-century architect Andrea Palladio in the neighbouring valley of the Brenta.

Timber domestic and farm buildings also show their own local styles of construction and decoration. For instance, in Friuli haylofts have semi-decorative side panels of diagonal wooden slats, of a type seen nowhere else in the Alps, whereas in the German-speaking areas of Asiago and Gressoney the provision of copious flowerboxes full of geraniums takes priority.

The common practice throughout the Italian Alps of mixed arable and cattle farming does, however, produce broad similarities in the traditional agricultural implements used and the arrangement of a typical village house. The ground floor of the house is a cattle shed, the first floor with its balcony is for human habitation, while the second floor is a well-ventilated hayloft protected by very broad eaves. Sometimes, when the slope of the ground is steep enough, hay is loaded into the loft from the hillside across a short bridge. It can then be easily thrown down from the other side into a waiting cart.

One thing must be said about farming which is a sad reflection on post-war Italy. All the way from the Lake of Orta in the west to Garda in the east – the fashionable and picturesque playground of the Milanese – the once-productive fields have been neglected. Terraces have gone wild, vines ramble over broken pergolas, fruit trees full of dead wood for lack of pruning yield little fruit or have ceased to produce any crops at all. The peasants have gone to work in the factories of Turin and Milan, so the colourful vegetable market at Omegna sells nothing locally grown. Nobody cares, least of all the new immigrants from Calabria and Sicily, or the tourists windsurfing on the lakes.

The Alpine chapel at Isolello on the banks of the Sesia. The frescos on the façade and the *trompe l'oeil* pilasters are typical of painted decoration on buildings in Val Grande.

Tourism developed in the western and central Italian Alps towards the end of the nineteenth century, and to this day you can still travel from Milan to five lakeside termini on the only remaining private railway system in Italy, the *Ferrovia Nord Milano*. Aristocrats, professional men and wealthy industrialists from Milan vied with each other to build their villas in picturesque spots overlooking the lakes. Steamboat quays, electric tramways, promenades and fountains were all constructed to amuse the visitors to the stylish new hotels. The more discerning travellers of the time loved Val Gressoney. There Queen Margherita, widow of Italy's King Umberto I, built Château Savoie in 1900–04; it is now a museum.

Not just the countryside, but some of the towns too have the air of being forgotten. For example, Omegna on the Lake of Orta and Porto Ceresio on Lake Lugano were Milanese lakeside resorts developed at the turn of the century, but they have now gone to seed. Varallo, in Valsesia, has been able to keep its old-fashioned character thanks to a bypass which keeps the traffic away.

Tourism can cut both ways. While it does wonders for the local economy, it destroys the very regional characteristics which some visitors, at least, come to enjoy. With the construction of bland pseudo-Alpine, or frankly modern, tourist facilities, the villages of Gressoney la Trinité and Barzio near Lecco have ruined themselves.

The official philistines are also at work with the written word. There exists a guide to the plateau of Asiago which completely fails to mention that the people speak a kind of German and have kept their own culture independent of Venice since the eleventh century.

Walser costume of Gressoney

The Festival of the Madonna in Val Gressoney

This is a sample of the Val Gressoney dialect:

D'Lljiku Winnacht ischt a Virtag van d'Lljibu
Vrawa un wir sëin auch gcheemen bettun
un grüzen dëi Vrawa das nöit nua mat
n'ündsch wërre van gouschi un bloatri un
endri büedschi dinhi. Dschi ischt an vrawa
das wëlti noch n'ündsch tun bessur:
n'ündsch brinnhen as söiri hümmil in disch
weelt. Franh sua: war müssun nöit nuan

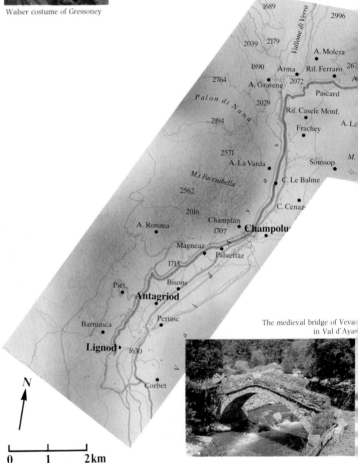

The medieval bridge of Veva
in Val d'Aya

lugun z'goan im hümmil wa war müssun
auch bettun un beitun das da hümmil
cheemi in disch weelt.
   Um dahümmil voat a wën war lien
n'ündsch liere van dëi Eju das wëlti
n'ündsch ellji wi dschëin Su: völli guz heers.

The French Speakers of Piedmont

In an Alpine arc from the Col de Mont-Genèvre to the
first of the lakes, Lago di Orta, Italy is ringed with
French-speaking valleys. To the west of this route lie
the Waldensian valleys near Turin, populated six
hundred years ago by religious exiles from Lyon and
discussed at length in our route called the Waldensians' Glorious Return. Next comes the area of Val
d'Aosta, at the point where the Alpine watershed
turns east. Here the culture is French and the

language has been kept up to date by good communications over the Little and Great St Bernard passes. After the Second World War the Italian Government acknowledged this separate identity by making Val d'Aosta an autonomous region.

Our route begins in the last of the area's French valleys. Val d'Ayas. Then, after a 30km (19 mile) interval of German speech in the Walser districts of Gressoney and Alagna, we re-enter a French zone in Val Sesia, outside the autonomous region, where Italian is more common. At the minor watershed between Varallo and Omegna we leave French speakers behind us.

The spire at Gressoney La Trinité

Typical Walser house at Gressoney La Trinité

Fra Dolcino and *The Name of the Rose*

Scopa church, which we pass on the road down from the village towards the river, recalls the violent times of the fourteenth century. A plaque on the building may be translated:

> On 24 August 1306 the bravest men of this valley agreed to draw up their ranks at this ancient church, of which the present chapel is the latest form. Here they joined the crusade against the heretical invader, *Fra Dolcino*, swearing before the sacred altars

Frescoed façade at Pedemonte

A romantic engraving of 1896 showing the St Gotthard pass

View of Riva Valdobbia in Val Grande

> they would never lay down their arms until the enemy alike of their liberty and their faith had been driven from the land.

The heresy of Fra Dolcino forms part of the background to the violent events of 1327 in Umberto Eco's masterly novel *The Name of the Rose* (1980) which take place in an unspecified monastery in the

Apennines some 100km (60 miles) south of Scopa. With the monastery sheltering former Dolcinians and with a papal inquisition about to arrive, the monks are all too afraid to satisfy the curiosity of the innocent narrator, a novice called Adso, until an old Franciscan friar tells him a story that began sixty years before.

Fra Dolcino, says the friar, was born a priest's bastard in the diocese of Novara, but began his career at Trent, preaching in the name of poverty against private ownership and proclaiming free love – he himself seduced the beautiful and noble Margaret of Trent. When the bishop drove them out, she joined an armed band of a thousand which headed west and was welcomed by the rebellious people of Gattinara, a town which stands just where the River Sesia flows out of the Alps into the plain. The promiscuous and ever-growing band, now called Dolcinians after their leader, Fra Dolcino, incited peasants and outcasts to rise up and exterminate their oppressors.

This was too much for the establishment. From Avignon in the winter of 1305 Pope Clement V proclaimed a crusade against the Dolcinians, now grown to three thousand, with a full pardon for all those joining the crusade. A series of massacres followed, and eventually Dolcino, Margaret and a few other survivors were captured and cast into prison at Biella, another town on the edge of the plain, between the mouths of Val d'Aosta and Valsesia. The Bishop of Biella had the lovers tortured all around the town and then burnt at the stake. Sentence was carried out on 1 July 1307.

The footbridge at Mollia

The church at Scopa where Fra Dolcino's heretics were defeated

An Edwardian balcony at Varallo

The Sacro Monte of Varallo

Varallo, the capital of Valsesia, is a town whose old-fashioned air is preserved by the modern by-pass. The main street of Varallo is named after King Umberto I, who was assassinated in 1900. It contains several fine shopfronts from that period. The street leads to the church of Sta Maria delle Grazie which contains a rood screen and a series of frescos depicting the life of Christ by the Valsesian artist Gaudenzio Ferrari (1484–1546). From here a footpath leads in twenty minutes to the summit (608m, 1995 feet) of the Sacro Monte, a centre of pilgrimage and the main point of interest at Varallo.

This 'New Jerusalem' was founded in 1486 by a Milanese nobleman and Franciscan monk, Bernadino Caimi. Building started in 1493 and continued until the late seventeenth century. The church dates from 1614–49, with a façade of 1896, and is surrounded by forty-five chapels which represent the holy sites of Jerusalem. The shrines were decorated by Ferrari and his followers with frescos and painted lifesize terracotta figures. Among the scenes of sacred history to be seen are the Magi and the Crucifixion, both by

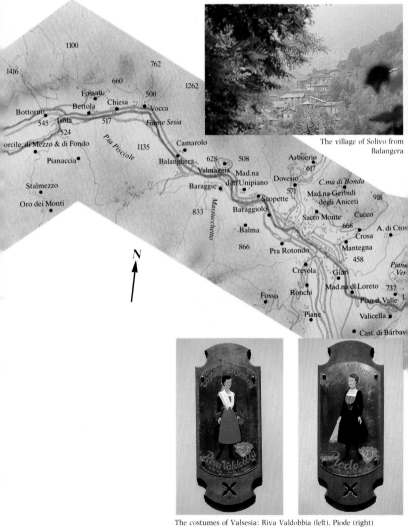

The village of Solivo from Balangera

The costumes of Valsesia: Riva Valdobbia (left), Piode (right)

Ferrari, and the Temptation by Giovanni Tabacchetti (c1555–c1635).

St Julius and the Lago di Orta

Orta is a beautiful little lake 12km (7½ miles) long, supposedly called Cusio by the Romans. At its head stands Omegna, a turn-of-the-century resort now gone to seed. Those few peasants who remain in the area come into town on market days wearing traditional dress.

The River Strona at Omegna

The historic interest of Orta centres on the graceful island. When St Julius came here from Greece in 379 to convert its people he at once selected the lovely site for a sanctuary. According to legend the boatmen refused to ferry him to the island for fear of the dragons and serpents living there. So, using his cloak as a sail and his staff as a rudder, the saint stepped on to the lake and was blown across to the island. There he blessed the evil reptiles, who leapt into the lake and were never seen again.

Julius's church of S. Giulio has been many times rebuilt, but the crypt preserves both his body and the enormous vertebra of one of the dragons. Modern scientific opinion assigns the bone to a whale. In the church is a pulpit of the ninth century with carvings of hideous beasts, probably those he drove out.

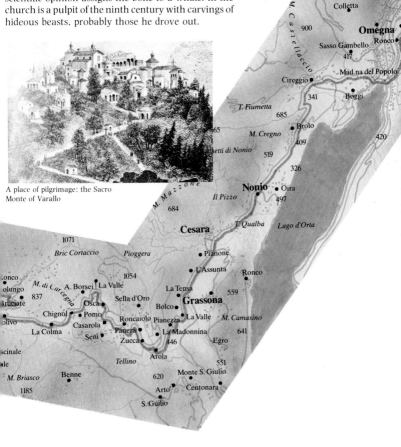

A place of pilgrimage: the Sacro Monte of Varallo

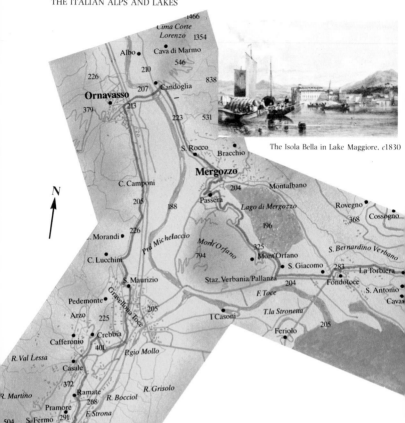

The Isola Bella in Lake Maggiore, c1830

A lakeside villa at Verbania

Lake Maggiore

Our path first passes the tiny lake of Mergozzo, once a bay of Lake Maggiore and the supposed haunt of smugglers between Piedmont, Lombardy and Switzerland. Like all the Italian lakes, Maggiore has a classical name – Verbano, which some authorities say is derived from Minerva, the Roman goddess of wisdom. The distinctive marks of Lago Maggiore are its splendid mountains and exquisite islets, although not all writers are polite about the islets.

As we cross the lake by ferry from Verbania to Laveno, Isola Bella lies among the Borromean Islands to the right. The English novelist Richard Bagot, who spent most of his life in Italy, comments in *Lakes of Northern Italy* (1907) on Isola Bella's 'monstrous artificialities', and goes on:

> The gardens, laid out in terraces in 1671 by
> Count Borromeo, are a triumph of bad taste.
> Artificial grottoes bristling with shells,
> terrible pieces of hewn stone, which it would
> be an offence to sculpture to term statuary,
> offend the eye at every turn. The vulgarity
> of the whole conception is redeemed by the
> luxuriance of the semi-tropical vegetation
> and the beauty of the views across the lake.
> The interior of the palace is little worth
> visiting: a gallery of very indifferent pictures,
> mostly palpable copies pompously labelled as
> Titian, Leonardo da Vinci *etcetera*.

Bagot's bitchiness may not be typical, for among those who were captivated by the beauty of this lake were the Emperor Napoleon I and Queen Victoria.

Verbania, on the Piedmontese shore, is a name, derived from the Latin, for a new commune which was created in 1939 by uniting the old settlements of Pallanza and Intra. The Swiss factories at Intra with their smoking chimneys led one Victorian writer to call it the 'Manchester of Maggiore'. In the same year a Captain McEachern gave his remarkable botanic garden at nearby Villa Táranto to the nation.

All along the shore can be seen the beautiful villas of the Milanese, some of them open to the public. When you land on the Lombardic side at Laveno you see a monument near the quay which commemorates an attempt by the Garibaldians to take the town from the Austrians during the *Risorgimento* in 1859. But compared with Lake Como, Maggiore is remarkably lacking in tales of political intrigue and military activity.

A view on the Lake of Mergozzo

The church of Cabiaglio

Porto Ceresio and the Ambrosian Church

Porto Ceresio, named after the Roman corn goddess Ceres, is another Omegna, a turn-of-the-century Milanese lake resort rather gone to seed. The waters of Lago di Lugano, also known as Lago Ceresio, are said to be among the most polluted in Europe.

The parish church of Porto Ceresio is dedicated to St Ambrose (c339–397). The interior, decorated in an extreme Baroque style, is the scene of the north Italian rites of the Ambrosian Church. The Ambrosians hold a doctrine slightly different from the Roman Church, maintaining that every believer can have direct access to God without the intercession of a priest. They were founded by Ambrose, Bishop of Milan from 374, and their rites are still largely confined to Lombardy.

Ambrose was governor of the province of Aemilia-Liguria. When the Bishop of Milan died in his capital, Ambrose was advanced by his congregation from

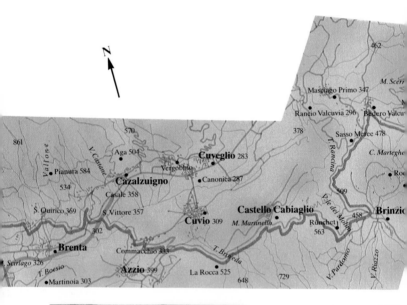

The cloisters of the church at Ganna

baptism to the bishopric in just a week! He proved himself an audacious man, standing up resolutely to the Emperor Theodosius I who had the blood of seven thousand Thessalonican rebels on his hands. Ambrose is also remembered for giving the world a famous dictum. When the mother of St Augustine came to Milan from North Africa she complained that Christians there did not fast on the Sabbath as in Rome and her homeland. Ambrose advised her: '*Si fueris Romae, Romano vivito more; si fueris alibi, vivito sicut ibi*' – When in Rome, do as the Romans do; when you are elsewhere, live as they live elsewhere.

Sunset on Lake Lugano

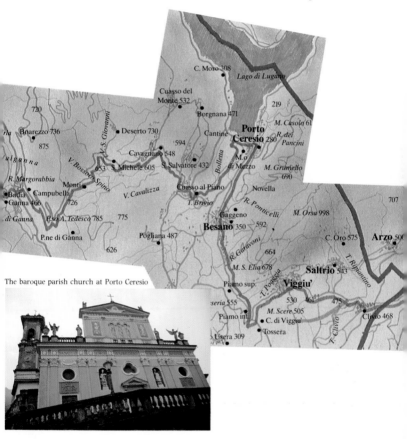

The baroque parish church at Porto Ceresio

The Most Famous Firemen in Italy

Many visitors to the little country town of Viggiù are puzzled to find on sale in the newsagents postcards of ancient fire engines manned by old-fashioned crews. The reason is a popular song of the 1950s *I Pompieri di Viggiù* (The Viggiù Firemen), recorded by the Trio Lescane. The crews were extremely dashing, the lyrics assure us, and full of bright ideas. One crew decided to pump petrol instead of water on to the blaze. Even this folly did not prevent the girls' hearts missing a beat as the firemen raced past on their engine.

Limited Border Opening at Roggiana

The border post at Roggiana near Vacallo operates during rush hours only. At this point only pedestrians, and possibly cyclists, may cross from Switzerland into Italy, and they are limited to two periods – 7 till 9 in the morning, and 4 till 6 in the afternoon.

The crossing is a footpath which is physically barred to motor vehicles. An alternative all-day border crossing lies just 2km ($1\frac{1}{4}$ miles) to the south.

A Taste of Switzerland

Between Porto Ceresio and Chiasso our route makes a brief detour into Switzerland, the Italian-speaking canton of Ticino. At the first village, Ligornetto, there is no apparent difference in the language or the design of the buildings and their state of repair, and the only obvious signs of Switzerland are a statue of Justice and a Ristorante Federale. In the countryside, however, it is abundantly clear that we have left Italy, for here the fields of tobacco, maize and vines are neatly tended and not an acre is wasted.

Como from Brunate, showing how the Roman street plan is preserved in the centre of the town where Pliny was born

Italian detail at Ligornetto   A peasant girl from Como (1927)

The Como School of Masons

Along this route through the Alpine foothills of Lombardy can be seen many village churches which have been rebuilt several times. The interior is likely to be Baroque and sometimes, as at Porto Ceresio on Lake Lugano, the decoration achieves a riotous character reminiscent of Spanish Baroque.

During these rebuildings the church towers seem to have been held more sacred than the ancient naves and have been preserved in their original style.

The path from Laveno on Lake Maggiore to Lecco on the south-east arm of Lake Como is punctuated by well-built Romanesque campanili. The characteristic finishing touch to these bell-towers is a copper onion dome, a rather Tyrolean feature; more rarely a Baroque statue crowns a tower which was rebuilt during the Renaissance.

A Renaissance statue of Pliny the Elder in its niche on the façade of Como cathedral

The Romanesque examples have survived for eight centuries because they were built by the celebrated Como school of masons. These craftsmen earned such an excellent reputation that they were employed not just in Lombardy, but as far away as Tuscany.

If you want to inspect the quality of their stone, its

working and superb jointing, an easily accessible example of their masonry can be found in the fourteenth/fifteenth-century south-east tower in the city walls of Como itself. The stonework looks so fresh that one can at first be deceived into thinking the tower had been heavily restored in the nineteenth century. The church towers of the Como masons are so numerous that they can easily be found without directions.

Apse of S. Fedele at Como

The path reaches Lake Lecco

Lecco and Alessandro Manzoni

That branch of the lake of Como which extends southwards between two unbroken chains of mountains, and is all gulfs and bays as the mountains advance and recede, narrows down at one point, between a promontory on one side and a wide shore on the other, into the form of a river; and the bridge which links the two banks seems to emphasize this transformation even more. . . . Lecco . . . lies on the lakeside not far from the bridge, and is even apt to find itself partly in the lake when this is high; it is a big town nowadays, well on the way to becoming a city. At the time of the events which we are about to describe, this township was already of some importance; it was fortified, and so had the honour of housing a commandant.

So begins one of the most famous of all Italian novels, *The Betrothed (I Promessi Sposi)* by Alessandro

A panoramic view of Lecco dating from 1896

Manzoni, first published at Milan in 1827 and here translated by Archibald Colquhoun.

The action is set during the Thirty Years' War (1618–48) and takes place largely in Lecco, with interludes at Milan and in the surrounding mountains. Superficially it is a story of the trials in the love between the innocent peasant girl Lucia and her silk weaver Renzo. Throughout the book the peasants behave more nobly than their betters, such as Count Rodrigo of Lecco.

At one point Renzo gets caught up in bread riots at Milan and narrowly escapes capture by the authorities, while Lucia flees Lecco and the attentions of the count to find unexpected help from the ruthless Visconti. He later reforms, reflecting the author's own conversion to the Church before he wrote the tale.

Manzoni ensured that all the historical detail was relentlessly accurate, and revised the book with the help of a Florentine governess to make the language consistent with correct Tuscan speech. So it became an important literary instrument in the unification of Italy, and to this day is, unfortunately, forced on Italian schoolchildren at the too tender age of nine.

To an adult it is indeed a splendid read, and a much deeper book than at first appears. Some of Manzoni's contemporaries saw it as an attack on the Church, particularly in the craven character of Don Abbondio, the very soul of a spineless priest, while others who lacked the author's eye of faith found it anti-Italian. One wrote that 'Its perpetual preaching of forgiveness and of resignation to the Divine Will seem like submissiveness to slavery and the negation of patriotism, and make *I Promesi Sposi* into the Book of Reaction'.

A view at Colle Balisio

The monument at Lecco to the
novelist Alessandro Manzoni
(1896)

A distant view of Valtorta village

The Italian Lakes

This ancient pathway has now reached a point halfway through the Italian lakes. How were they formed? They all share a common origin during the last glaciation, which ended about ten thousand years ago. Each glacier carved out a deep U-shaped valley for itself and carried the debris along with it. At the foot of the glacier the rubble was released from its icy trap and deposited in a terminal moraine, or ridge of stones stretching across the valley. When the glaciers finally retreated the moraines formed effective natural dams, and so we have the lakes.

Prehistoric people settled around the lakes and particularly around Lake Como. This is probably due

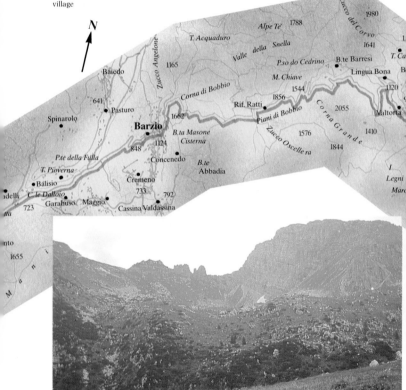

Zuccone-Corna seen from Piani di Bobbio

to the fact that the easiest of all trans-alpine routes comes right up to the head of the Inn valley, over the Maloja pass (1815m; 5955 feet) and down to the Lake of Como. The last stage of the journey was made by water using a unique type of square-rigged ship which still survives in use.

In the last century, when the lakes became the playground of the Milanese and the European bourgeoisie, there developed a railway network which is unique: the *Ferrovia Nord Milano* is the only remaining private railway company in Italy. Little known is the internal navigation system which also links some of the lakes. Canals extended from the basin of Dàrsena on the River Olona in Milan. The *Naviglio Grande* reached the River Ticino and Lake Maggiore, the *Naviglio di Pavia* connected the Ticino and Po rivers, while the *Naviglio della Martesana* led to the River Adda and Lake Como.

Painted Buildings in Valtorta

As you descend from the lonely plateau of Pian di Bobbio you find that the Brembana valley resembles Val Sesia in fostering a tradition of painting the outside of houses and churches. The first place, Valtorta, at the head of the valley, would be quite picturesque enough even without a proliferation of frescos. The village is a sheer delight, with almost every old house displaying wall paintings perhaps up to two hundred years old. They represent both figures and *trompe l'oeil* architectural details.

Inside the church of La Torre, a hamlet near Valtorta, are well-preserved medieval frescos of the Christmas story and lives of saints, while outside is painted St Christopher. Paintings embellish all the villages in the upper part of the valley. At Cassiglio the Milesi house displays the dance of death: Death himself leads out two old people in chains. There are other notable frescos on houses at Olmo, Piazza Brembana and Lenna. This last village has an Etruscan name,

St Christopher, Valtorta church

Typical external decoration on a Valtorta house at Cassiglio

and was probably founded in this safe retreat by Etruscans driven from the Po valley by Celts.

At this point our route turns east via Foppo into Val Secca, but only a little way down the main valley from Lenna lies Camerata, ancestral home of the Tassi family. Omodeo de'Tassi was the founder in 1290 of a postal system and was an ancestor of the Princes of Thurn and Taxis, German postmasters-general.

Clusone

Clusone is the commercial and tourist centre of the upper Serio valley, situated at the centre of a picturesque plateau which climbs to the Presolana pass, 647m (2122 feet) above sea level. Its name may be derived from the Latin *Clusum*, referring to the narrow gorge which the River Serio cut through the foothills of Monte Cimitero. The origins of Clusone are extremely ancient: already in Roman times there was a large commercial quarter where the tradesmen congregated, bringing arms from the surrounding valleys. The armoury was both the arms store and the residence of the captain of arms, who had a dual function as the custodian of the armoury and

The baroque church of Roncobello in Val Secca

governor of the valley. The first document in which the name of Clusone is mentioned dates from 830.

During the period of Venetian domination of this area Clusone, at the request of the local inhabitants, retained a Venetian vicar, rather than being subject to Bergamo, as was the custom for all the neighbouring parishes. In the early nineteenth century Clusone was an important centre of the iron industry: much of the crude iron ore from the Scalve valley was brought for smelting in its furnaces.

Among the notable buildings in Clusone is the town hall, dating from 1008, with its remarkable planetary clock constructed in 1583 by a local horologist, Pietro

Fanzano. It indicates the height of the Sun above the horizon, the length of the night, the solstice, the constellations traversing the Sun, the daily position of the Moon in relation to the Sun and the Earth, the year, the month, the day, the hour and the minute.

The parish church of Santa Maria Assunta, built in 1688 and designed by Giovambattista Quadrio, contains a number of fine works of art, including a fifteenth-century font, the high altar designed by

(*Top*) The Chiesa di Disciplini at Clusone

(*Bottom*) The Palazzo Municipale at Clusone in Val Seria (1898)

Andrea Fantoni, and a painting of the Ascension by the eighteenth-century Venetian artist Sebastiano Ricci. Quadrio also designed the Palazzo Fogaccia, dating from the end of the seventeenth century, which has extensive internal murals, and a fine collection of furniture dating from the seventeenth and eighteenth centuries.

A distant view of the village of Ardesio in Val di Serio

Val Camonica's Prehistoric Rock Carvings

Val Camonica was for many centuries the most important centre of Alpine rock art, engraved on boulders worn smooth by glaciers. Students have so far discovered more than 180,000 engravings. The only comparable site is Monte Bégo near Col de Tende in the Alpes Maritimes, where 40,000 images were engraved during the Bronze Age; they are dated between 1800 and 1400 BC.

The abundance of carvings in Val Camonica has only been realized since 1956, when the Israeli archaeologist Emmanuel Anati began research in the area and founded the *Centro di Studi Preistorici* in Capo di Ponte. Despite Anati's work it is still not clear why this valley was favoured by artists from the Late Stone Age to the Roman invasion, apparently expressing their devotion in votive pictures to their deities.

The engravings represent humans, gods, animals, scenes from everyday life, ploughs, vehicles, houses, weapons and scenes from battles. Unlike those at

Boats on Lake Iseo at Lovere

The castle at Esine in Val Camonica

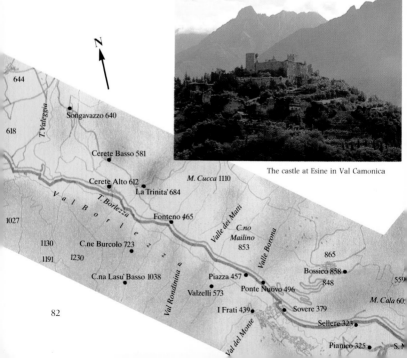

N

644

618

T. Valeggia

Songavazzo 640

Cerete Basso 581

Cerete Alto 612

T. Borlezza

La Trinita' 684

Val Borlezza

M. Cucca 1110

1027

Fonteno 465

Valle dei Matti

C.no Mailino 853

Valle Borona

1130   C.ne Burcolo 723

865

1191   1230

Val Rondinina

Bossico 858

848

559

C.na Lasu' Basso 1038

Piazza 457

M. Cala 60

Valzelli 573

Ponte Nuovo 496

I Frati 439

Sovere 379

Val del Monte

Sellere 323

82

Pianico 325   S. N

Monte Bégo these engravings are quite accessible: the most prolific site is near Capo di Ponte, a few kilometres further up the valley from Breno. It has been made into a national park (the Parco delle Incisioni Rupestri). There thousands of images can be seen at close quarters, 900 alone on the Naquane rock. Other random examples can be found on boulders all over Val Camonica. The carvings are explained in the Museo Didattico at Capo di Ponte.

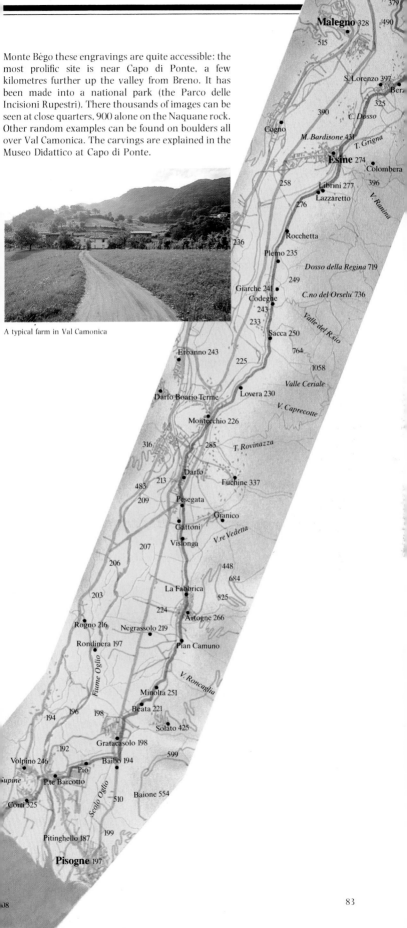

A typical farm in Val Camonica

Malegno 328
286
379
490
515
S. Lorenzo 397
Berz
325
390   C. Dosso
Cogno
M. Bardisone 431   T. Grigna
Esine 274
Colombera
258   Librini 277   396
Lazzaretto
276
V. Ramina
236   Rocchetta
Plemo 235
Dosso della Regina 719
249
Giarche 241   C.no del Orselu' 736
Codeghe
243
233   Valle del R sio
Sacca 250
764
Erbanno 243   225
1058
Valle Ceriale
Darfo Boario Terme   Lovera 230
V. Caprecotte
Montecchio 226
316   285   T. Rovinazza
Darfo
483   213   Fuchine 337
209   Pesegata
Gianico
Gattoni   V.re Vedetta
207   Vislonga
206
448
684
La Fabbrica
203   525
224
Rogno 216   Negrassolo 219   Artogne 266
Rondinera 197   Pian Camuno
V. Roncaglia
Fiume Oglio
Minolta 251
Beata 221
194   196   198
Solato 425
192   Gratacasolo 198
Volpino 246   Baibo 194   599
Pio
upine   P.te Barcotto
510   Baione 554
Corti 325
Scolo Oglio
Pitinghello 187   199
Pisogne 197

08

Lago d'Iseo

The Romanesque church at Capo di Ponte in Val Camonica

Val Camonica seen from the road to Passo Crocedomini

Lake Idro: Retreat of Fugitives

Edgcumbe Staley dwells upon the romantic remoteness of this small and beautiful lake in *Lords and Ladies of the Italian Lakes* (1912):

> With something akin to relief the wayfarer comes upon the mountain Lago d'Idro, a stretch of deep indigo-dyed water, clear and cold as a cheerless tarn. The eye fastens upon the Rocca d'Anfo, hanging dizzily over the gloomy waters – once a Venetian fortress, a prison in later days, and now a ruin of the gory past. From Verona, Mantua, Cremona, Brescia and Bergamo, many a fugitive made a dash for liberty in the fastnesses of the Val Sabbia. Witches were hailed to the mountains, there to expiate their crimes by the sword or starvation. Many a luckless princeling and many a maiden forlorn hid where the wild torrent Caffaro splashes foam on the dank rocks. In the impassable gorge discovery was impossible. . . .

Prehistoric carving at Naquane

Idro, the *Lacus Eridius* of the Romans, supplies a grim contrast of scenery with its smiling neighbours, the lakes of Iseo and Garda. Despite its small size – it is only 9km (6 miles) long – its waters reach the remarkable depth of over 270m (900 feet).

Pliny on the Italian Lakes

Pliny the Elder (Gaius Plinius Secundus) was born in Como in AD 23, and died in 79 while trying to observe at close quarters the eruption of Vesuvius which destroyed Pompeii. Book III of his *Naturalis Historia* contains this description of his native country:

> The tenth region of Italy [Gallia Cisalpina] also contains eleven famous lakes and the rivers of which they are the source, or which, in the case of those that after entering the lakes leave them again, are augmented by them – for instance the Adduam [Adda] that flows through Lake Larius [Como], the Ticinum [Ticino] through Lake Verbanus [Maggiore], the Mincium [Mincio] through Lake Benacus [Garda], the Ollium [Seo] through Lake Sebinus [Iseo] and the Lambrum [Lambro] through Lake Eupilius [Pusiano] – all these streams being tributaries of the Po.

M.ga Valle Orsaccia
S. Antonio
Corno della Tor
1411
M. Tonolo 1535
S. Barbara
Darzo 408
Ermos
Rio Riccomassino
M. Macaone 1437
Dos del Fo
F. Chiese
Basso
Bresandi 388
Rose Vaghe
Prespede
Cast. di Lodrone
Dosso Anses
Roverset
Cerreto
755
Lodrone 392
S. Rocco
Riccomassimo
Castagneta
Palade
Fle. Gadoli
Paradisi
F. Caffaro
Bornighe
Le Pozze
Ponte Caffaro
Cantarane
Campini
Bruto
R.lo delle Pozze
Pian d'Oneda
Monte Suello
S. Giacomo
Bondone
Camping
Refino
R. Lo Campadello
1635
R.lo Benini 951
Communale
C. Lombardi
Prato della Fame 374
Posale
864
Reconda
902
anela 1815
Piana dei Bandi
C. Zanzini
Rio della Bega
Tornione
Corna Pagana 1455
M. Breda 1503
Plagna 545
Residence S. Antonio
lla Berga 1527
Forte di Cima Ora 1535
S. Antonio
T. Liperone
a 1480
Cime Baremone 1776
Cima dell'Ora 1539
Scalvini
a Spina 1521
La Spina
1442
1290
Cima Valcaei 1374
Camping Marina
Legria
Baitoni
Spina
Roccolo
Plonka
1495
C.ma Meghe 1801
1208
F. le Garepione 1136
Cuca Chetoi 895
C.ma Fontana Fredda
Cima Cereto Chetni 926
Zoia
Tese di Sopra 792
920
T. re
M. Censo 1012
Casali 461
Tese di Sotto
237
M. Porle 1342
S. Petronilla
P.so Cucca Bassa 1020
Lago Didro
Anfo

The Lake Dwellings of Northern Italy

Everybody knows that Venice is a city built upon piles. But how many visitors to the lagoon realize that the Venetians were following a building tradition thousands of years old? The remains of prehistoric lake dwellings have been found in Italy on the shores of Lakes Como, Maggiore, Garda, Idro and Ledro, at several sites in the plain of the River Po, and also on the banks of the rivers Dora Riparia and Dora Baltea.

The best place to study these wooden buildings is the Lake of Ledro. On the east side near Molina you can see about 15,000 wooden stakes when the water level is low. They date from the early Bronze Age (c1800 BC)

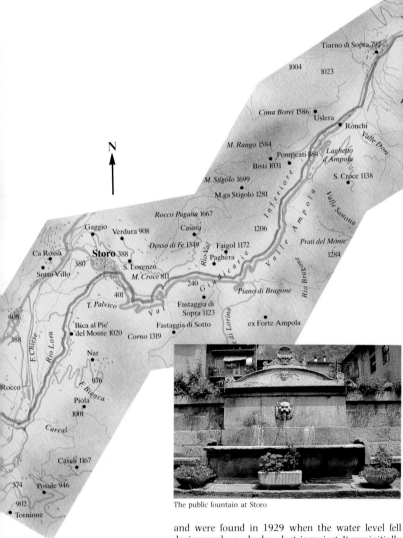

The public fountain at Storo

and were found in 1929 when the water level fell during work on a hydro-electric project. It was initially thought that, like similar structures at Neuchâtel in Switzerland, the dwellings were built in the waters of the lake for defence, but it is now known that they actually stood on the marshy foreshore.

A reconstruction stands in exactly that position near the excellent little museum, which illustrates the discovery of the dwellings and draws attention to similar lakeside villages still inhabited today in central Africa, Indonesia, Madagascar, Amazonia and New Guinea. The museum displays a wide range of artefacts which came from the dwellings, including pots, bronze vessels and tools, metal and amber jewellery, stone arrowheads and bronze weapons: in all, an extremely good cross-section of a typical Bronze Age settlement.

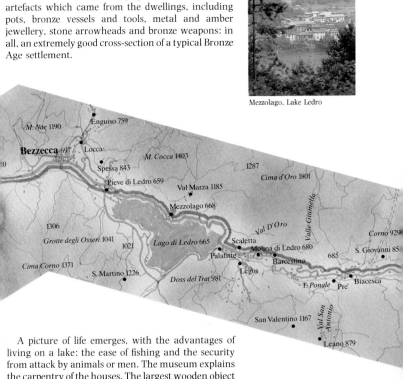

Mezzolago, Lake Ledro

A picture of life emerges, with the advantages of living on a lake: the ease of fishing and the security from attack by animals or men. The museum explains the carpentry of the houses. The largest wooden object is a dugout canoe, 4.5m (15 feet) long, carved from a single trunk of fir. A comparable canoe has been found near the Lake of Ampola, not far from Ledro.

Reconstruction of a prehistoric lakeside dwelling at Lake Ledro's museum

The town square in Storo

Venetian Galleys carried to Lake Garda

The transport of battle fleets across land is recorded at least three times in antiquity: by Hannibal at Tarentum, by Dionysius I across the Isthmus of Motya and by Nicetus across the Isthmus of Corinth. During the war between the ascendant Venetian Republic and the Visconti, Dukes of Milan, an even more impressive enterprise of this kind took place. In 1438 the Venetians needed a plan for regaining control of Lake Garda, and so relieving their city of Brescia, as well as the villages along the lake shore. A Greek sailor, Niccolò Sorbolo, came up with a scheme.

A fleet composed of twenty-five ships and six galleys was taken up the river Adige to its highest navigable point. From there the vessels had to be dragged 24km (15 miles) overland on mountain tracks. For this purpose 2000 oxen and a complementary corps of labourers were employed. Engineers cleared the ravines, built bridges and levelled roads and finally got the fleet to the top of the pass of Monte Baldo. Then

N

M. Tombio 841
Varone
Pernone
T. Albola
T. di Varone
Ischia   Pasine
V. Maria   Albola   S. Nazzaro
Rocchetta 1521   Riva   Alboletta   S. Giorgio
Cast. Rocca   Grez   Grotta
M.ga Vasotina 929   Sabbioni   Alessandro
S. Giovanni 858   Brione   M. Brione 376
Biacesa   Giaconi
Lago di Garda (Benaco)
Pregasina
Belvedere   Naveselle

Arco
Stadio
Conv. dell'Adda
C. Bruttagosta
Capit Narzelle   C. Noreda
249   S. Nicolò
M.so dei Dossi
Dosso della Costa
C. Perrini   240   426   609
S. Luigi
Ischiana   M.ga
Carpenada   M.ga Treni
Le Marmitte   C. Gobbi
dei Giganti   Fiavei 902   M. B.
Busata
Vignolo
Nago   Giresole
Rov. Castel   S. Tommaso   S. Ro
Penede   Campadello 682
S. Giuseppe   Capp. dei Signori 752
Torbole
Alveo Lago di Loppio
M. S. Gius 748
528   Nagrolle
Carpeneda
F. Sarca

The waterfront at Riva on the northern end of Lake Garda

began a tricky descent, with the ships restrained by ropes attached to rocks and trees and lowered slowly by capstans. After fifteen days and at a cost to the Republic of 15,000 ducats the fleet reached Torbole without mishap. But the expense and effort were in vain, for the Milanese rushed up a fleet and blockaded the invaders in the habour at Torbole. The Venetians, nevertheless, granted a pension of 500 ducats a year to Niccolò Sorbolo.

Eugenio di Savoia, Rovereto

The frescos and church of S. Rocco near Pannone

The War Museum at Rovereto
From the beginning of the sixteenth century until 1918 Riva and Rovereto belonged to Austria: the border crossed the north end of Lake Garda about 6km (4 miles) from Riva. The campaign which annexed the territory to Italy is commemorated by Italy's main First World War museum in the castle at Rovereto. The bulk of this fortress was built about 1300, and was reconstructed in 1488 after a siege. Much of the medieval work remains, and the sixteenth-century

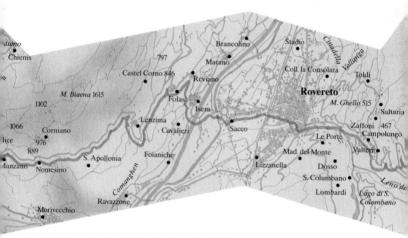

Venetian historian Cardinal Pietro Bembo attested to its defensive strength by describing how 60 Venetians held the fortress for 37 days in 1487 against a force of about 30,000 Austrians.

All aspects of the First World War are covered by displays in a series of twenty-nine rooms in the museum: artillery, aviation, civilian internees, Italy's allies, the rôle of the German-Austrian alliance, the Red Cross, and Italy's dashing regiments, the Alpini, Bersaglieri and Arditi. Outside the town is the enormous Bell of the Fallen, the largest in Italy, which tolls every evening for the dead of all nations.

The mountain resort of Serrada

German-speaking Cimbri on the Asiago Plateau

Go into the cemetery of the parish church at Luserna and observe the strange names of the families: Nanc, Castellan, Paolaz, Moz, Poiarach, Chelle, Maroder, Neff and Baiz are some examples. These are the 'Cimbri' people who make up the so-called Sette Comuni (seven communes) here on the Asiago Plateau. They speak a language which is incomprehensible to both Italians and Germans: a sample is quoted overleaf.

Although the Cimbri were for long the butt of Italian jokes, twentieth-century Germans have taken them more seriously. When some Cimbro men were captured in the First World War one of their Austrian captors, Eberhard Kranzmayer, became interested in their language, for it is in many ways a frozen form of medieval German. In the Second World War Bruno Schweizer took an interest and wrote several books, but we should be warned about his ethnic conclusions as he was a member of the 'Cultural Commission of the Third Reich'.

There is documentary evidence that a group of peasants from the west of Upper Bavaria migrated towards Verona during a period of famine in about 1050. The Tredici Comuni (thirteen communes), the

German lines to the church tower at Luserna, rebuilt 1919

other Cimbro area near Verona, probably contains the descendants of these people and is therefore the older of the linguistic 'islands'. The settlement by Bavarians of the Sette Comuni probably dates from around 1120. From about 1150 the Asiago Plateau became the power base for the Ezzelino family.

The history of the Cimbri is a little difficult to trace because documents say nothing about the language or the nationality of the inhabitants. From 1404 to 1797 Venice ruled the Sette Comuni, quite benignly it appears, for on 30 November 1417 the Doge Tomaso Mocenigo confirmed their ancient privileges. On the other hand the Austrian régime installed in 1815 after the fall of Napoleon did practically nothing to preserve

The arms of the Cimbro town of Luserna: crossed mason's hammer and cold chisel

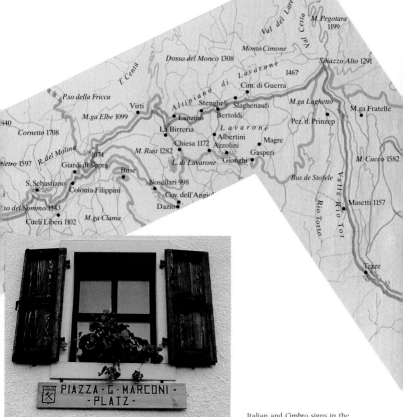

Italian and Cimbro signs in the main square of Luserna

the Cimbro culture. The people responded by feeling more and more Italian. During the revolution of 1848 a 'Legione Cimbrica' rose with the Venetians to cast off the Austrian yoke. A few Cimbri were found among Giuseppe Garibaldi's One Thousand in the liberation of Sicily. Finally in 1866 the Austrians were defeated and the area became Italian. From that time scholars began to study this area and its folklore.

The plateau suffered terribly during the First World War: artillery destroyed almost every building. There were several battles including one on 15–16 June 1918 involving the British XIV Corps.

By this time the cultural revival of the Cimbri had begun. Asiago itself, for instance, was rebuilt in a totally German way and all the parish churches have vertical proportions and tall spires.

Little Red Riding Hood's Meeting with the Wolf

This is a sample of the Cimbro dialect of the Asiago plateau, taken from the 1985 calendar of the *Kulturverein Lusern* (Trent).

Ma in in balt hat s bokhennt in bolf, bodas hat gevost bo s geat. S diarndle hatten khöt ena tzo vörtase, ke s is nó tzo giana ka dar nòna. Intânto as hat àugelest röasla vor di nòna, dar bolf is gânt bahemme in haüsle vo dar nòna.

Apena gerift hattar geklopft afti tür, un hat khöt: ≪ I pin s Roat baritle ≫. Di nòna hat offe getànt di tür, kontent tzega s khinn.

A paved road at Bisele on the plateau of Asiago

Battle of Asiago war memorial

Ena tzo khòda a bòrt dar bolf issar gesprunk adosso un hatze gevrèsst in an ũantzege mumpfl.

An ur darnò ista gerift s Roat baritle un is darschrakht tzega offe di tür. S diarndle is gänt in bahemme tzega bas da is vürkhent. Nämp in pett is darschrakht segante in schnabl vo dar no'na asò gebèkslt.

S diarndle hat gegloabet, ke s is khent peen in beata boda hat di nòna. Un hat gevorst: ≪ Nòna vobas hasto a sötta groases maul ≫. Dar bolf hat respundart: ≪ Tzo vressade pessar ≫.

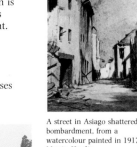

A street in Asiago shattered by bombardment, from a watercolour painted in 1917 by Martin Hardie

A 'Klondyke' scene at Sta Zita on the plateau of Asiago

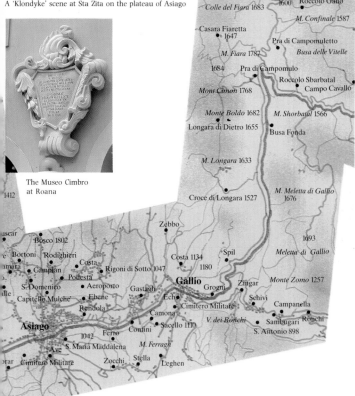

The Museo Cimbro at Roana

Colle del Fiara 1683
1722
1600 Roccolo Gano
M. Confinale 1587
Casara Fiaretta 1647
Pra di Campomuletto
M. Fiara 1787
Busa delle Vitelle
1684 Pra di Campomulo
Roccolo Sbarbatal
Mont Cimon 1768
Campo Cavallo
Monte Boldo 1682
M. Shorbatal 1566
Longara di Dietro 1655
Busa Fonda
M. Longara 1633
M. Meletta di Gallio 1676
1412
Croce di Longara 1527
Zebbo
1693
uscar
Bosco 1802
Meletta di Gallio
Bortoni Rodìghieri
Costa 1134
Spil
Costa
imara Campian
Rigoni di Sotto 1047
1180
Podestà
S. Domenico
Aeroporto
Gallio
Monte Zomo 1257
Gastagh
Zingar
ille Capitello Mulche
Ebene
Ech
Grogni
Schivi
Rendola
Camona
Cimitero Militare
Campanella
Asiago
Sacello 1110
V. dei Ronchi
Sambugari Ronchi
1042 Ferro Confini
S. Antonio 898
Ave S. Maria Maddalena
M. Ferragh
rar Cimitero Militare
Zocchi Stella
Leghen

THE ROMAN ROADS OF NORICUM

Follow My Legion

When the Roman legions conquered the Alps they created the province of Noricum in the eastern section of the region. This route follows the Roman roads for 270km (168 miles) from their provincial capital of Virunum, near Klagenfurt, through the regions of Carinthia, Styria and Salzkammergut to Iuvavum, now Salzburg.

Although the route runs through some spectacular gorges none of its three passes is more than 1250m (4100 feet) above sea-level, so this ancient pathway remains open to travellers for more of the year than others in this book.

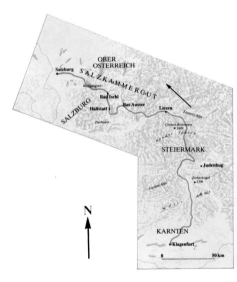

Since it also follows small country roads for nearly the whole way it is in all respects the best of our routes for cyclists.

In Austria no one expects to see Roman road surfaces in use today. But interesting Roman remains and vestiges of Roman times can be seen not only in local museums but at the very roadside and incorporated into later buildings.

The Roman approach to Noricum began in the second century BC, after the defeat of the Carthaginian invasion of northern Italy led by Hannibal (the exact route across the Alps which Hannibal – and his elephants – took has never been finally settled by the historians). Once the Carthaginians had withdrawn, the Romans set about reoccupying the plain of the River Po. This led to the founding of the Adriatic port of

Aquileia on the north-eastern edge of the plain in 183–81 BC. This was a decisive event for the exploitation of the mineral resources of the Alps, for it opened up friendly trading relations with the Celtic *Regnum Noricum* (Kingdom of Noricum).

A Roman relief carving in the gardens of the Kärntner Landesmuseum at Klagenfurt

So along a prehistoric trading route which linked the Baltic Sea (see the Amber Route, page 120), amber, iron and gold began to reach Aquileia, which grew as a result of this trade to be the fourth largest city in Italy after Rome, Milan and Capua. In Noricum the main trading place was at the large Celtic settlement on the Magdalensberg, to which pioneering Roman traders penetrated as soon as Aquileia was founded as a base from which they could operate.

For their part the Celts wanted Italian-manufactured goods, especially bronze objects and the fine red pottery known as Arretine or Samian ware. Surprisingly enough, the bibulous Celts also developed a strong partiality for Mediterranean wine, in spite of the high cost of carrying it over the Plöcken pass or Saifnitzer-sattel.

An independent Noricum remained beneficial to both Celts and Romans for more than 150 years. Only after Augustus emerged victorious from civil war in 27 BC as Rome's first emperor did it seem expedient to 'pacify' the whole Alpine chain instead of just controlling the passes which led through to Gaul in the west.

In 16 BC Augustus abolished the sovereignty of Noricum at a stroke, and the Celtic Noricans were realistic enough not to argue. As a result, they were given a special status not accorded to other provinces such as neighbouring Raetia (which included the Tyrol and parts of present-day Bavaria and Switzerland). In practice this status meant that the Noricans could keep their own rulers, the Roman garrison was comparatively small and enlistment of local people as auxiliaries in the Roman army was not enforced.

During the next few years the Romans extended the Empire across the Alpine foreland as far as the Danube. At last the Empire had a naturally secure frontier in this wide, slow-flowing river, for any artificial boundary drawn among the complex of Alpine ridges had always been vulnerable to outflanking if intrepid barbarian invaders chose to use the lesser-known passes.

Only in AD 45 did Noricum become a full province. After so many years of the *Pax Romana* the fortifications of the capital of the Celts on the sacred hill of the Magdalensberg became unnecessary. The Roman governor established his new capital, Virunum, at a much more convenient spot in a broad valley, though still within sight of the old Celtic city.

The surrounding valleys of the Drave and Glan rivers became heavily Romanized and densely settled. Virunum was well placed on a major crossroads for both military and economic control of the province. The north-south road, called the Norican Main Highway, connected Italy with the new frontier towns along the Danube and carried goods to and from the unconquered tribes of Germany as well as Noricum itself.

In its most developed form in the third century AD the Roman road network was highly efficient. The whole system was run by the army, with each sector under the control of a senior officer; the Christian martyr St Florian was one of them. Stations at regular intervals supervised the traffic and provided changes of horses for the imperial post. Hostels were built to shelter the travellers, who could pray for fair weather and a safe journey at wayside shrines.

It was the custom of travellers pausing at the shrines by the mountain passes to dedicate small bronze votive tablets carrying short personal inscriptions. Surviving tablets help us to see who used the Alpine roads. The passers-by included troops of all ranks journeying to or from their stations on the frontier, merchants of every kind (including slave dealers), magistrates and other officials of the Empire travelling about their business, Roman and provincial ambassadors, as well as the occasional aristocrat on a sightseeing tour or a historian in search of material.

Although many roads in the Alps could carry only trains of mules, those sure-footed animals famous for their work in mountainous conditions, most roads were upgraded in due course for wheeled traffic. Vehicles included the *plaustrum*, the ordinary wooden cart; the *carpentum*, the fast two-wheeled van used by the Imperial post; and the *carruca*, a heavy luxury carriage. A covered four-wheeler of the last-named type is shown in a relief carving from Virunum, now built into the wall of the church at Maria Saal, near Klagenfurt. It is said to have been possible to rest, converse or dictate letters in such a carriage (though it apparently had no springs) and Julius Caesar is reputed to have written a book in a carriage while crossing the Alps.

The Romans built their vehicles to a standard wheel-gauge of 1070–1100mm (42–43 inches), and the roads were constructed to suit this width of vehicle. But the four-wheelers, whether heavy, lumbering freight wagons or luxury carriages, had one thing in common: no steering. They had to be skidded around corners by brute force, and the Roman engineers had to build their roads with easy curves.

Although they did not think of steering, the Romans were imaginative when it came to constructing mountain roads; they never tried to make them straight in the Alps. Steep gradients held no terrors for the engineers.

Where a modern road needs perhaps twenty-two hairpin bends to reach a pass, the Romans sometimes managed with only two.

One almost ludicrous example has been found on the Maloja-Julier pass in Raetia. One eight-metre (twenty-six-foot) section climbs a slab of rock at a thirty-degree slope, with steps cut to assist the wagoners and draught animals. They would certainly never have managed to climb it at all without the four deep holes provided in the rocky side walls for the insertion of levering bars.

The most spectacular Roman road building in the Alps occurs in narrow defiles. The road, carefully sited at a height which minimizes the work, is cut into the cliff with an overhanging roof of rock or built up on arches which cannot be seen from the road itself. Tunnels are driven through the most difficult spurs, but are never more than a few metres long.

Panorama of Salzburg towards the dramatic silhouette of Hohensalzburg, former stronghold of the prince-archbishops

Although the road network is fairly familiar to historians from surviving itineraries, particularly a map now in Vienna known as the Peutinger Table, it is usually the general route rather than the exact line of the road which is known. For in the Alps landslides, avalanches and spring floods soon obliterate human handiwork.

So in the following pages we follow an authentic Roman route, but at any given place it remains a matter for lively conjecture whether our steps fall on a concealed Roman surface or not. That said, we trace the Norican Main Highway past known Roman posting stations from the provincial capital for some 140km (87 miles) towards the frontier of the Empire. We cross the River Mur at such a station, called Ad Pontem, but on reaching the River Anisus (now the Enns), we branch off on a lesser-known Roman road through the Salt Gap at Pürgg to the ancient mining towns of Hallstatt and Salzburg.

The route has been chosen partly because it has historic interests other than those of the Roman period. In particular it passes Lake Hallstatt, close to which lies the type-site of the Iron Age Hallstatt Culture, and it climbs the Magdalensberg, where the Celts had their capital long before the Romans arrived.

Turning to more modern times, Bad Aussee is an attractive and unspoilt old town where church-going, brass bands and traditional costumes are an unselfconscious part of everyday life. Bad Ischl was rebuilt as an aristocratic spa in the nineteenth century after the Austrian emperor Franz Joseph II made it a fashionable resort by building a palace nearby – so fashionable in fact that for four months of the year it was the social centre of the old Austro-Hungarian Empire.

A Roman milestone from Noricum

Virunum: Site of the Provincial Capital

When Noricum became an official Roman province in AD 45 under the Emperor Claudius, the new governor and his staff were unwilling to live high up on the Magdalensberg and perhaps be snowed in for months on end. The authorities in Rome agreed and gave orders for a new city, Virunum, to be built at the foot of the mountain.

The site of Virunum is now called the Zollfeld. It is a large and level arable field bisected by a farm track and

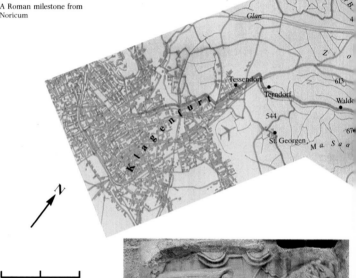

A Roman traveller's coach in a tomb relief on Maria Saal church

flanked on either hand by coniferous woods. No Roman remains can be seen there (except for some stonework built into the wall of a nearby farmhouse), but in its day the town possessed all the essentials of urban living: temple, theatre, amphitheatre, public baths, municipal buildings, paved streets, a public water supply and dwelling houses built around courtyards.

Virunum lasted as a full capital for only about 150 years, for at the end of the second century AD the administration moved to Ovilava (now Wels), close to the legionary commander at Lauriacum (Lorch). Only the finance department remained behind. Then in about AD 300 Noricum was split into two provinces, and Virunum became a capital once more, this time of Noricum Mediterraneum. About AD 400 the garrison of the Norican *limes* (frontier) ceased to receive regular pay, the barbarians flooded in, Virunum was abandoned and its buildings collapsed. Nobody ever reoccupied a site so difficult to defend.

The Magdalensberg: a Tribal Capital Gone Roman

The Alpine Celts built their towns on hills. Their *oppidum* (administrative centre) on the summit of the Magdalensberg (1058m, 3471 feet) was the capital of Noricum before the Roman occupation. A farmer ploughing there in 1502 found the life-size bronze statue known as the Youth of Magdalensberg. The original, now in Vienna, is thought to be a Roman copy of a fifth-century BC sculpture by Polycleites; it may have been a gift in about 50 BC from the Adriatic traders at Aquileia to their colleagues in Noricum. Copies can be seen in the Klagenfurt and Magdalensberg museums.

About 100 BC Roman merchants, thought to be mostly representatives of the great republican

Norican pottery. Magdalensberg

A Roman of Hadrian's time

Memorial to a Roman called Publicius of Virunum

business houses, crossed the Carnic Alps to found a trading settlement below the native town on a terrace 920m (3018 feet) above sea level. The shops of the merchants surrounded a *forum* (market place) frequented by native craftsmen and traders. This site has been thoroughly excavated.

Most of the impressive remains which visitors see today are imperial buildings put up after the peaceful Roman annexation of Noricum in 15 BC. The natural terrace was enlarged to form a larger square with buildings on all four sides, including an assembly house and administrative building with a central temple raised on a podium. Pottery and metalwork – Norican iron was famous in the ancient world – are displayed all over the site.

Business here was so good that the little trading settlement developed into a real town with richly decorated houses: some merchants adorned their houses with lavish frescos of Minerva, Venus, Iphigenia and Dionysus, painted, indeed signed, by masters from the Mediterranean.

Oxen drawing a hay-sled in Carinthia (1891)

A castle dominating the river just before Eberstein

The Romans in the Görtschitz Valley

Our road goes north from Magdalensberg amid rolling hills through the province of Carinthia (Kärnten). The first pass that we cross is the Perchauer Sattel beyond Neumarkt; it is about 95km (60 miles) from the start of the route in Klagenfurt. Somewhere in this valley in AD 113 a group of Germanic and Celtic troops defeated the Romans, the first setback suffered by Roman troops in Noricum.

The churches and other old houses in the villages repay careful examination, because the people have often built ancient carved stones into the walls for display, not just as building stone or rubble. The

The Norican goddess Noreia at Wieting

A Carinthian couple on a path in 1930

church at Maria Saal, being so close to the capital Virunum, has numerous pieces of sculpture in its south wall. They include a tombstone carved in relief which shows a four-wheeled Roman travelling coach. The vehicle is drawn by two horses, and there is a window in the covering. Such a vehicle would be used by a magistrate or senior army officer. It was probably in a coach like this that Julius Caesar is reputed to have written a book while crossing the Alps. The church at Hüttenberg has two Roman altars in its walls, while at Wieting, where the Romans had an important iron mine, a headless statue stands right beside the road, probably representing the native goddess Noreia.

Hüttenberg and the Norican Iron Industry

It was probably the fame of Norican iron that attracted the first traders over the Alps from Aquileia. The main mines were at Hallstatt, around Neumarkt and in the Görtschitz valley around Hüttenberg and Wieting. All these places are on our route.

Recent experiments with a reconstructed furnace on the Magdalensberg have achieved a temperature as high as 1420°C (2588°F), quite sufficient to produce steel. Tools made in Noricum are certainly no different from modern steel and it seems clear that Norican iron owed its reputation to this high quality.

Hüttenberg was one of the major Norican mines and was as important a smelting centre as Magdalensberg itself. The mines remained public property for the

A memorial to the Roman Iuventius Vibenus, Hüttenberg church wall

most part, and it was common for Roman army officers to be seconded to manage them. There is evidence for the presence of Roman officers at Feldkirchen, 50km (30 miles) east of Hüttenberg.

Two altars, now built into the wall of Hüttenberg parish church, are further evidence of Roman activity.

St Margarethen, the possible site of Noreia

The Roman Goddess Noreia

Five ancient writers, including Pliny and Strabo, mention the place-name Noreia, but scholars have argued about its location for more than a century; using the classical itineraries one could search for Noreia anywhere along the Norican Main Highway between Virunum and Neumarkt.

The innocent mountainside village of St Margarethen am Silberberg is as good as any, or so the

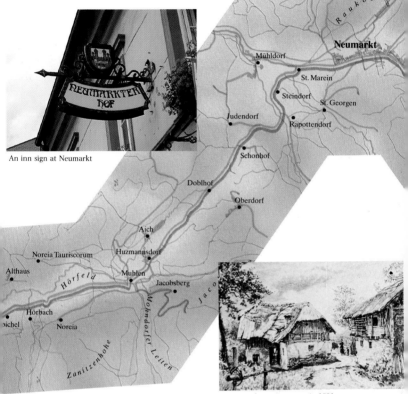

An inn sign at Neumarkt

A country scene in 1891 near Zollfeld, site of Virunum, Roman capital of Noricum

Austrians seem to think, as they have recently renamed it Noreia. We found it difficult to agree, as the site has not even been excavated.

What is certain is that Noreia was the native goddess of the pre-Roman Norican kingdom. And at the village of Wieting in the valley south of St Margarethen we find her statue. Seated right beside the Roman road is a headless marble figure of third-century date, with a dedicatory inscription. She is either Noreia or the Mother Goddess, and some authorities on Noricum consider the two deities to be one and the same.

A wooden hut similar to an Iron Age house, St Margarethen

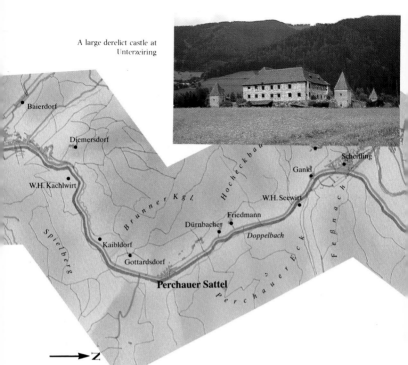

A large derelict castle at Unterzeiring

Baierdorf
Djemersdorf
W.H. Kachlwirt
Brunner Kgl
Hocheckbau
Scheifling
Gankl
W.H. Seewirt
Spielberg
Kaibldorf
Dürnbacher
Friedmann
Doppelbach
Feßnach
Gottardsdorf
Perchauer Eck
Perchauer Sattel
Perchauer

→ Z

A typical onion dome at
St Georgen

The Norican Main Highway

The most important road in the Roman province was the Norican Main Highway, the northern extension of the vital trade route from the Adriatic port of Aquileia. After ascending the Tagliamento valley, it crossed the Carnic Alps and Norican frontier by the Saifnitzer-sattel, a low pass also called Pontebba and Camporosso, only 812m (2664 feet) above sea-level. Passing Santicum (modern Villach), it skirted the north shore of the Wörthersee to the later Roman capital at Virunum (the Zollfeld). It then passed north over the Neumarkter Sattel, the Niedere Tauern and the Pyhrn Pass to Ovilava (Wels) and the frontier fortress at Lauriacum (Enns-Lorch) on the Danube.

If it had not been for the unsympathetic presence of modern trunk roads in the north we would have followed this route all the way to the Empire's frontier. As it stands our Roman road traces the Norican Main Highway for some 140km (87 miles) from Virunum across two passes to Liezen on the River Anisus (now the Enns), before taking a minor branch to the ancient centres of Hallstatt and Iuvavum (Salzburg).

Crossing the River Mur

You cannot find a more descriptive place name than *Ad Pontem*, At-the-Bridge, where the Roman road crosses the River Mur. The settlement is now called Lind, but you will be disappointed if you look for evidence of the Roman crossing here. The oldest bridge remains you can see are some concrete abutments apparently blown up in the Second World War. The Romans had another crossing at St Georgen (also called Judenburg) 6km (4 miles) downstream; the church there has one of the largest red onion domes to be seen in the Alps.

In the face of a political and military crisis the Emperor Diocletian (reigned AD 284–305) tried to stabilize the Roman Empire by completely reorganizing its administration. In Noricum his radical reforms divided the province into two, using as a natural geographical boundary the mountains running from east to west. The new frontier, which we cross at the smooth pass called Hohentauern, ran along the high ridge of the Niedere Tauern which forms the north side of the Mur valley. The division was in force shortly before AD 305, and the new provinces were called Noricum Ripense, meaning along the banks of the river (Danube), and Noricum Mediterraneum.

A fortified gateway at the town of Unzmarkt

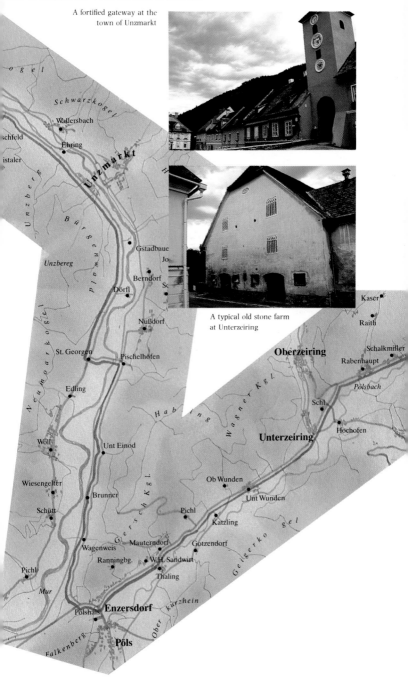

A typical old stone farm at Unterzeiring

The Cult of St Florian

St Florian was a martyred Roman soldier (Florianus) whose cult is found along the Roman Roads of Noricum and along the Amber Route where it follows the Via Claudia Augusta. He is the patron saint of Upper Austria and of fire stations.

The highly organized Roman road network was run by the army. Florianus became commander of the system within the frontier province of Noricum. His misfortune was to reach the high rank of *princeps officiorum* during the persecutions of the Emperor

The road to Hohentauern

A tiled roadside shrine of the Roman martyr St Florian, dated 1828

Diocletian. He seems to have betrayed his secret adherence to the Christian faith by helping some imprisoned Christians.

After Florianus refused to sacrifice to the Roman gods his persecutors tied him to a large stone and threw him into the river Enns near Lorch on 4 May 304.

Benedictine monks later built a monastery called Markt St Florian over his tomb, and his cult is centred around relics preserved there in the crypt. The monastery, considered one of the finest baroque buildings in Austria, treasures paintings by Hans Holbein and Pieter Bruegel, and can claim Anton Bruckner among its more recent organists.

Because of his watery end St Florian was originally invoked by victims of floods and those threatened by flooding. Early representations show him with the attributes of a millstone, a shield, a sword and a

THE ROMAN ROADS OF NORICUM

banner. About the fourteenth century he became associated with fire, for reasons which are not clear.

As we trace his images from the medieval to the modern period his military costume changes from a suit of armour to become a more and more authentic Roman uniform.

Devotees of the saint often sought his aid with this decidedly unchristian prayer: 'Good St Florian, spare my house and rather burn my neighbour's.' From being invoked against the threat of fire St Florian became the patron of fire stations and fire-fighting.

His saint's day is celebrated on 4 May and his cult may be found from Bavaria through Upper Austria into South Tyrol. When studying ancient highways it is particularly interesting to observe that the cult of this one-time commander of Roman roads is concentrated along the arteries of the Roman road system in his province.

A window at Trieben dated 1874

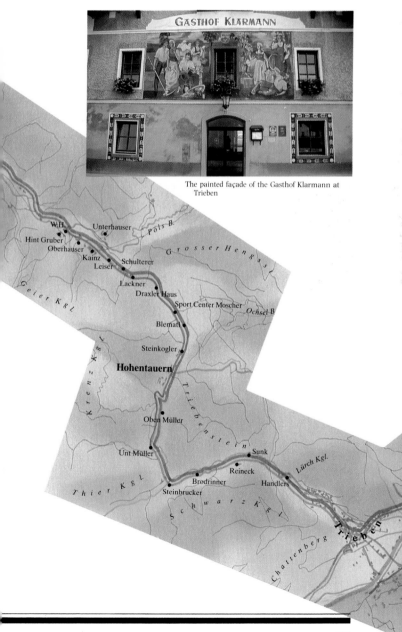

The painted façade of the Gasthof Klarmann at Trieben

Rottenmann town gate (inside)

Crossing the River Enns

The River Enns, known to the Romans as the Anisus, cuts in a narrow gorge through the north-eastern ranges of the Alps, called the Hohe and Niedere Tauern. The Norican Main Highway, running from the provincial capital of Virunum near Klagenfurt to the Danube fort of Lauriacum (now Lorch) on the frontier of the Roman Empire, crosses its last two passes on either side of the Enns: the Hohentauern (1250m, 4100 feet) and the Pyhrn Pass (945m, 3100 feet).

A significant tombstone has been found near Rottenmann. It belonged to a serving soldier in the Legion xv Apollinaris, based from AD 14 at Carnuntum (now Bad Deutsch Altenburg) further down the Danube. The tombstone proves that the Norican Main Highway was used as a natural road long before the Emperor Claudius (reigned AD 41–54) ordered its upgrading.

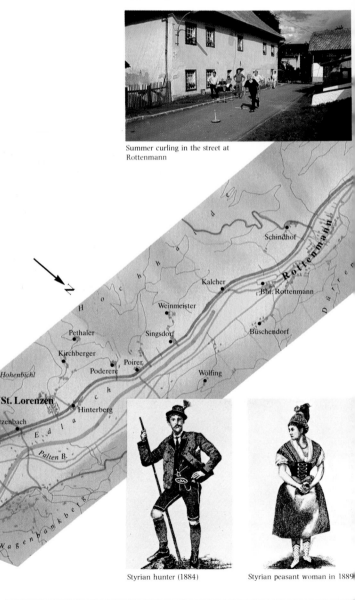

Summer curling in the street at Rottenmann

Styrian hunter (1884)

Styrian peasant woman in 1889

The Roman Army

The basis of the Roman army was the legion, a unit of about 5000 well armed and highly trained soldiers. Under the Empire each legion was divided into ten cohorts, each of six centuries. It will be seen that the century, originally – and nominally – one hundred strong, in reality consisted of about eighty men.

Each century was commanded by a centurion, and these officers were the backbone of the army. Most of them were promoted from the ranks.

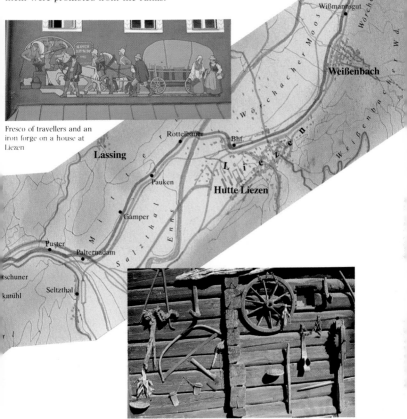

Fresco of travellers and an iron forge on a house at Liezen

Old agricultural implements preserved on a barn wall at Rottenmann

The size of the Roman army varied over the years, but for the first two hundred years of the Empire it never dropped below twenty-five legions or rose much above thirty. For a long time the biggest force was stationed along the Rhine, but in the early 100s AD the garrison guarding the Danube frontier was increased to twelve legions to keep out the barbarians who were massing along the north bank of the river.

In addition to the legions the Romans had locally recruited auxiliary forces under Roman commanders. Each legion had a force of auxiliaries attached to it, many of them specialist fighters such as archers. The auxiliaries consisted of cavalry contingents known as *alae* and foot-soldiers organized in cohorts – which were the same as the *cohors* of the regular legions – the size of these units varying between 500 and 1000. For many years auxiliaries made up the main garrisons of both Raetia and Noricum.

Serving in the Legions

Under the rule of the emperors, service in the legions of the Roman army was open only to Roman citizens. After a time, however, there were just not enough Italian-born Romans to man the legions, and it became necessary to recruit local men to serve. The answer was to give recruits Roman citizenship on appointment.

Service was for twenty years, with five years in the reserve. During his service the legionary was not allowed to marry, but of course the men cohabited

A view to the south from Schloss Trautenfels

A roadside shrine at Obersdorf

N

with their women just the same.

After he was discharged, with a handsome gratuity, the legionary generally settled in the civilian part of the camp where he was last stationed.

Auxiliary troops served for twenty-five years. They did not have Roman citizenship, and they received much lower pay than the regular soldiers. On discharge the auxiliary soldier also received a gratuity, plus a *diploma* which gave him Roman citizenship. More than 200 of these *diplomas*, which were pairs of bronze tablets, survive. Citizenship was highly prized since it conferred on the possessor voting rights and social status which were denied to other peoples living under Roman rule.

Pürgg: The Salt Trade as a Key to Power

About 900 BC the climate of central Europe deteriorated, becoming colder and more humid. This had a direct effect on the need for salt, whose real importance lay not in seasoning food but in preserving meat. In the new climatic conditions pickling in brine replaced air drying and salt joined iron as a key to economic power. Hallstatt, 40km (25 miles) further along our route, and Hallein, south of Salzburg at the end of it, both owed their immense wealth in the Iron Age to their salt mines.

While discoveries at both these mines tell us a great deal about how the salt was won from the ground, it is

A roadside shrine dated 1828   A rare surviving example of a Roman road in the Alps (Val d'Aosta)

not clear how much refining was carried out. Probably the high-grade salt required no purification for its basic purpose of conserving meat and fish. The consumption per head must have been high. The Roman writer Cato tells us in his *De Agri Cultura*, written about 160 BC, that every member of a household used one bushel of salt (10.4kg; 23lb) each season. There is scanty evidence of where this salt was consumed, but we can be sure that quantities of it were traded down from the mountains through the 'salt gap' at Pürgg to the area around Klagenfurt.

The arms of Bad Aussee

Country Traditions at Bad Aussee

Traditional costume is frequently worn throughout Carinthia and Styria, but especially in Bad Aussee, the capital of the Salzkammergut area, where church attendance is exceptionally high by current European standards. The town is the home of the *Erzherzog-Johann-Kapelle*, one of the famous folk-dress brass bands of Styria, and after Sunday morning service when the band is playing in the park the folk museum seems to have come alive.

The men attend in knee-breeches and short, bright green jackets, while the women's dresses all have tight embroidered bodices contrasting with generous white sleeves.

In its heyday Bad Aussee was a high-altitude spa 659m (2162 feet) above sea-level; its waters contain sodium sulphate. The little town had a social *Kurhaus* or pump-room, and three bathing establishments

[MAP]

N

called *Kaiser Franz-Josefs Bad*, *Vitzthum* and *Kur Anstalt Alpenheim*.

Today the town is better known for its exceptional opportunities for walking in the surrounding mountains and around their picturesque lakes, the Altaussee See, Grundlsee, Toplitzsee and Kammersee. The 1911 Baedeker says:

> The beautiful Toplitzsee, one and a
> quarter miles long, with two waterfalls.
> About a quarter of a mile farther on lies
> the sequestered Kammersee, in a grand
> situation at the base of the Tote Gebirge.
> This *Drei-Seen-Tour*, or tour of the three
> lakes, makes a very charming excursion.

The old part of the town is full of historic buildings. The first object to catch our attention was the wrought iron inn sign on the fifteenth-century *Blau Traube*, or blue bunch of grapes. There are two medieval churches, but unlike others earlier in our route neither seems to preserve any Roman carvings in its structure. The formerly monastic Spital-Kirche is a small chapel crammed with works of art, including a good early German winged altarpiece of 1449 and a statue of St Christopher, the patron saint of travellers. The parish church of St Paul was begun in 1300.

Bad Aussee's centre is at the Chlumetzkyplatz, a cobbled market place surrounded by interesting Gothic and later buildings. Of greatest importance is

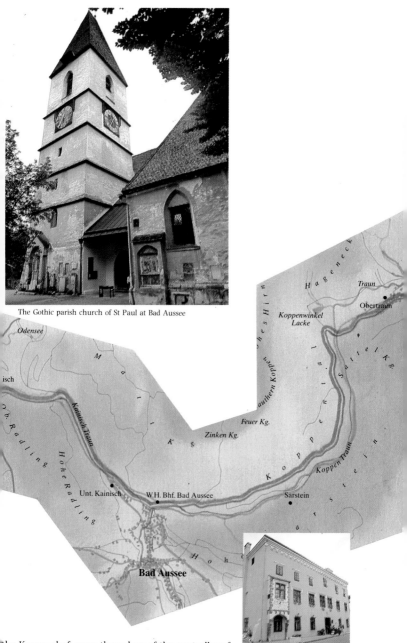

The Gothic parish church of St Paul at Bad Aussee

The museum at Bad Aussee

the Kammerhof, once the palace of the controller of mines. It sports splendid seventeenth-century red marble window frames with cable mouldings, and over the main door are the arms of Styria and the Habsburgs. Today the building houses the local museum, where there is a particularly good series of displays on traditional methods of salt-mining and transport in the area. These show, among other things, that the techniques of the nineteenth century were remarkably similar to those employed in the Iron Age at nearby Hallstatt.

Hallstatt: Salt Mines and the Early Iron Age

The town of Hallstatt is famous to Austrians for its great scenic beauty and to the rest of the world for its place in prehistory. Its story concerns salt, the 'white gold' which was once so valuable and is now so common. On 1st April 1734 salt miners stumbled across the well-preserved body of a man dressed in skins and literally pickled in salt. As a pagan he received a very rough reburial at the hands of the

Hallstatt seen in 1889
from the railway
station across
the lake

The placid waters of Lake
Hallstatt with the town on the
far shore

superstitious Christians who found him.

Then in 1846, in the early days of archaeology, the manager of the mine, Johann Ramsauer, began a stupendous series of excavations in the undisturbed burial fields of the Salzberg valley, 350m (1150 feet) above the Hallstätter See. The sheer number of graves – more than two thousand were excavated in the next fifty years – and the richness of the grave goods ensured that the term Hallstatt Culture passed into the language of Europe. The Hallstatt period is the same as the Early Iron Age (900–450 BC), just as the La Tène period (named from a prolific find-spot on Lake Neuchâtel) is the same as the Late Iron Age (450–1 BC)

Salt attracted the Romans here from AD 13 to about 476. They moved the settlement down from the Salzberg to a site near the present village on the steeply sloping banks of the deep blue lake. In picturesque 'modern' Hallstatt, where some of the wooden houses have stood for five hundred years, you can study the Iron Age, the salt mines and the story of the village. Two museums, prehistoric and local, stand close to the market square. You can also visit a salt mine. In the Middle Ages the mine continued to be so valuable that the Rudolfsturm was built in 1284 to protect it. In 1595 the Austrians began to improve the mine by laying what we may call the world's first pipeline. When fully developed a conduit carried brine 35km (22 miles) past many boiling plants to Bad Ischl and Ebensee.

Salt mining remains the most important source of income for the people of Hallstatt, although blasting operations are now restricted for fear of damaging evidence of the ancient workings. This unique setting attracts not just archaeologists, but also people interested in field sports, winter sports and mountaineering. To preserve the village the Austrians have driven a bypass through a road tunnel behind it.

Bad Ischl: an Emperor's Summer Resort

Dr Wirer von Rettenbach, a Viennese physician, first brought the therapeutic waters of Ischl to public notice in about 1820, and as Bad Ischl it soon became a highly fashionable summer resort. During its heyday before the First World War Baedeker described its medicinal facilities in the guide to *The Eastern Alps*:

Besides the salt-baths (which contain 25

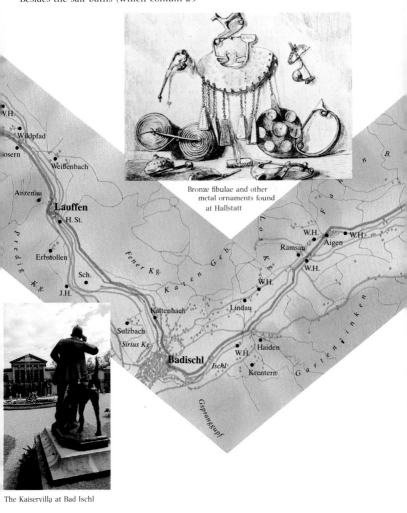

Bronze fibulae and other metal ornaments found at Hallstatt

The Kaiservilla at Bad Ischl

per cent of salt) there are mud, sulphur, pine-cone, vapour, and other baths, in addition to the whey-cure and the saline and sulphurous drinking springs.

Central to taking the cure here are the spacious old Trinkkur, or pump-room, of 1831 and the modern Kurmittelhaus.

The place took the fancy of the Emperor Franz-Josef, who ruled Austria-Hungary for close on seventy years from 1848 to 1916. His family and the Imperial Court took up residence there each year from July until September, enjoying not just the baths but also the renowned shooting and hunting in the heart of the Salzkammergut.

Just to the north of the town, on the banks of the River Ischl, Franz-Josef built the neo-classical Kaiser-

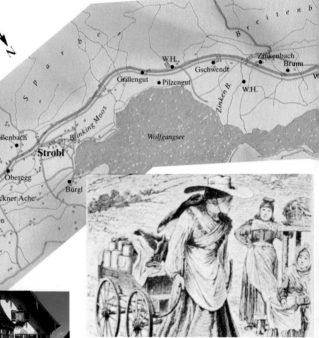

An Upper Austrian peasant girl carrying milk to market in 1889

Mozart and the Rathaus, St Gilgen

villa in an extensive landscaped park. The grounds include a small marble château, the Marmorschlössel, used as a retreat by the Emperor's wife, the Empress Elizabeth, in much the same way as Marie-Antoinette used the Trianon at Versailles.

Many famous characters are associated with this town, among them the ill-fated Emperor Maximilian of Mexico who was born here in 1832 but ended his days before a firing squad of the Mexican Republic in 1867 (Goya painted the scene). In the grounds of the former Hôtel Rudolfshöhe Johannes Brahms and the Empress Elizabeth are commemorated with monuments. Other composers who lent their talents in the days of Ischl's splendour include Anton Bruckner, Johann Strauss and Franz Lehar, whose villa has been arranged as a museum. Plays are performed again in the old court theatre, now renamed after Lehar.

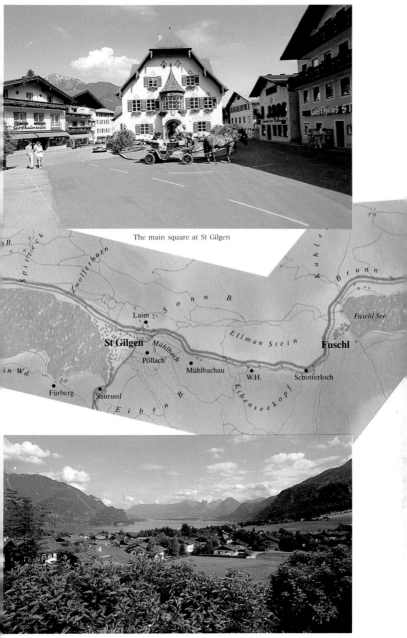

The main square at St Gilgen

A distant view of St Gilgen and the Wolfgangsee from the west

The Gothic Altar at St Wolfgang

The Wolfgangsee is a beautiful and fashionable lake within easy commuting distance of Salzburg. The villages around it are innocent of any Roman connection. Of the resorts St Wolfgang lies on the north shore away from the main road. The sixteenth-century parish church there is an old centre of pilgrimage and possesses one of the finest examples of Gothic wood-working in the world. It is a winged altar, which Michael Pacher of Bruneck carved in 1481. When the wings are open you can see in the scene of the Coronation of the Virgin our old friend, the Roman martyr St Florian.

The baroque flavour of Salzburg

The Roman City of Salzburg

The very name of Salzburg, meaning salt town, marks the fact that it has, like Hallstatt, a long connection with the mining of salt. The link continues with the name of the river which flows through the city: Salzach is presumably a contraction of *Salzbach*, salt stream.

When the Romans founded their commercial centre of Iuvavum here in about AD 40 on the site of a Celtic settlement, Petena, the Salzach valley had already been occupied since the New Stone Age. The main part of Iuvavum lay on the left bank of the river, underneath the medieval city of Salzburg, with a minor town opposite on the right bank. Iuvavum was sacked by the Alamanni, a Germanic group of tribes who crossed the Danube in about AD 250. It took the Romans fifty years to restore order. The Alamanni

Roman finds from the Salzburg area

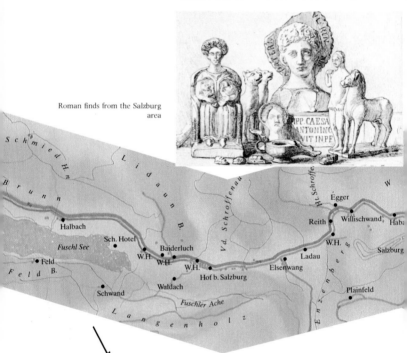

destroyed Iuvavum again when the Roman Empire collapsed two centuries later.

Unlike the Norican towns of Virunum, Teurnia and Aguntum, Iuvavum lies under a modern city and only small parts have been explored. Nevertheless there are three places where you can see the Roman period in Salzburg. The excavations under the cathedral display a villa and a temple to Aesculapius (Greek Asklepios), the god of healing, which was converted to a Christian basilica. The Toy Museum's courtyard contains a collection of Roman tombstones and milestones, while the most important discoveries are in the Museum Carolino Augusteum. Near Salzburg is the villa of a rich Roman landowner at Siezenheim, which contains one of the finest mosaics in Noricum, a second-century floor showing the legend of Theseus.

There is much more to Salzburg. A city cannot be the capital of the most powerful prince-bishop in southern Germany without leaving plenty of interest behind. And each summer Salzburg holds a festival in homage to its most famous son, Wolfgang Amadeus Mozart.

Roman tomb and milestones in the Toy Museum courtyard
at Salzburg

The Salzburg Festival

A view of the cathedral in Salzburg

The Salt Mines at Hallein

The town of Hallein, 20km (12 miles) south of
Salzburg, is in some ways another Hallstatt, for the
nearby hill of Dürrnberg was the site of a thriving Iron
Age salt mine. Production continued under the
Romans, and mining is still carried on there today. On
this site in 1932 Olivier Klose found a most exquisite
bronze jug. If you never see another Celtic work of art
in your life, go to see this one in the Museum Carolino
Augusteum in Salzburg.

THE AMBER ROUTE

Prehistoric trade from Bavaria to Venetia

The ancient pathway we call the Amber Route enters the Alps from the Bavarian plain, then strikes south straight across the widest section of the mountain chain through the Tyrol to a spur of foothills that points to the old Etruscan port of Spina, near Venice.

Some people might say that as an historic pathway it is a bit of a cheat, for though it is based on the prehistoric trade in amber, very few remains of that trade can be seen along the way, until you come to the end of the pathway at Este, near Padua. But it is a romantic route for all that, with plenty of historic sites, and there are good reasons for including it.

The ancient demand for amber in the Mediterranean lands far outstripped the local supply, so amber from the Baltic was imported. It either reached the northern Adriatic over the Alpine passes or was carried to the Dalmatian coast across the Danube, skirting the Alps to the east. When the Romans built the Via Claudia Augusta from Verona to Augusta Vindelicorum (modern Augsburg) in the first century AD they chose, as in so many parts of the Alps, to follow an earlier road. That road was the Amber Route.

From prehistoric times the beauty and mystique of amber made it one of the most highly prized materials. Stone Age people came under the spell of its lustrous russet colour and marvellous odour. Because they regarded it as a powerful talisman against evil their craftsmen carved it into amulets.

This superstition carried on into classical times; the Roman historian Pliny records that children wore such amulets around their necks. It was made into spindle whorls, to protect spinners against the evil spirits that might snarl their thread. Powdered amber was taken internally for stomach ailments. Mixed with honey and oil of roses, the powder was prescribed for ear trouble, and when mixed with honey of Attica it was regarded as a specific for failing eyesight. Oil of amber was taken to treat whooping cough and asthma, and was rubbed on the chest as a liniment.

The Greeks pursued amber avidly, calling it *electron*. From this name comes the word 'electricity' to describe another of its magical properties: when a piece of amber is rubbed it acquires a negative charge strong enough to attract small pieces of paper or thread.

This mixture of magic and specific carried over to the Middle Ages. For example, the

sixteenth-century writer Camillus Leonardus says in his *Speculum Lapidum* (1502):

> Amber naturally restrains the flux of the belly; is an efficacious remedy for all disorders of the throat. It is good against poison. If laid on the breast of a wife when she is asleep, it makes her confess all her evil deeds. It fastens teeth that are loosened, and by smoke of it poisonous insects are driven away.

The prehistoric site of Romagnano nestles at the foot of this limestone cliff between Trent and Rovereto

Amber was used as a fumigant, and the smell of its burning was thought to assist women in labour. It featured among the many powdered gems compounded into bezoar stones. These stones were cure-all lumps worn around the necks of the wealthy in costly pendant settings.

The scientific debunking of amber began in 1715 when the English physician and chemist Frederick Slare published his *Experiments and Observations upon Oriental and Other Bezoar Stones*. But you can find many people today who believe in the power of amber – and they are not all Baltic peasants trying to cure a headache!

Geologists classify amber as a fossil resin. It is derived from the sticky liquid that oozed from the bark of pine trees growing in the Tertiary period, about 60 million years ago. The hardened resin nodules were trapped and fossilized in the sediments that buried the remains of these primeval forests. Today the nodules can be found at the foot of cliffs that are undergoing active erosion, releasing the amber from its rocky tomb. Amber is found most abundantly along the Baltic coast, though some occurs in Italy, France and Spain, and further afield in Burma, Canada and the Soviet Union.

Amber is of great interest to entomologists and botanists because the sweet, sticky substance occasionally formed a perfect trap for a whole insect, which thus became fossilized, and leaves and small plants are also found preserved in amber.

However, unless your trusty dog sniffs out some amber in a field beside the path you will have to wait until you reach Este to see ancient pieces of the material. The archaeological museum in the castle there displays samples of amber jewellery traded along this route. They date from the thirteenth to the fourth centuries BC.

On the Italian side of the Alps you can tell you are following a Roman road not by its straightness but by the Roman place names along it, such as Prissiano and Appiano, and by the cult of the Roman martyr St Florian which is celebrated at churches along the way.

There were several cultural consequences of prehistoric trade along the Amber Route and highways parallel to it. For example, the

Etruscan script spread from Spina to the surrounding tribe of Veneti, who took it across the Alps into Germany. So when the Northmen of Scandinavia felt the need to make inscriptions they copied the forms of Etruscan letters which they found in use among north German tribes, and thus created runes. Going the other way, the influence of the Celts of northern Europe on the art of the Veneti can be clearly seen.

The Amber Route starts at Füssen in southern Bavaria. Nearby is the romantic castle of Neuschwanstein. It was built by the mad King Ludwig II of Bavaria in homage to the composer Richard Wagner, whose operatic characters crowded Ludwig's fantasies. A brilliant and tragic homosexual, Ludwig's mind was turned by unhappiness in love, and frustration at being made a puppet ruler within the new German Empire created by the Prussian statesman Otto von Bismarck. Ludwig, a strong swimmer, met his end by drowning himself in the Starnsee, incidentally drowning also his medical attendant, Dr Bernhard von Gudden, who tried to prevent the suicide.

One of the themes that this pathway traces is the change in architectural styles between northern Europe and the Mediterranean lands. As we travel south through Germany and Austria the historic buildings tend to display external frescoes and tall gables with spires or finials. Moving down the wedge of German cultural penetration into Italy towards the city of Trent, the style gives way to the Renaissance proportions of simple Italian houses, until by the time we reach Rovere della Luna the Gothic turrets and other northern 'nonsenses' have disappeared.

It is also significant to notice that in Rovere della Luna St Florian, whom we first meet on the Roman roads of Noricum in Austria, stops being the patron saint of the local fire stations. In art St Florian is always represented in the act of pouring water on a burning house.

Another theme is the exploration of castles. Among those on our route which are open to the public we draw special attention to Castle Tyrol above Meran and the fortresses at Trent, Rovereto and Este — the last-named not to be confused with Villa d'Este near Rome.

Incidentally, the names of Meran and Trent show the persistence of Germanic tradition in this area that was for so long under Austrian rule. On the Italian maps you will see them as Merano and Trento. But the locals stick to the old names, even for the roadside signs. Trent has its place in the history books as the venue for the Council of Trent, held from 1545 to 1563 to settle important questions of Roman Catholic dogma.

Our path comes down the whole length of the autonomous region of Trentino-Alto Adige, which is just the official way of referring to South Tyrol. After the unification of Italy, completed in 1871, extreme nationalists such as the poet and firebrand Gabriele d'Annunzio regarded South Tyrol and neighbouring Friuli as 'unredeemed territories' under Austrian occupation.

When the First World War broke out the Italians made it a condition of entering the conflict against Austria and Germany that Tyrol as far as the Brenner and Friuli passes would be taken from Austria and given to Italy once victory was won. The Alpine campaign of 1915–1918 has been overshadowed by the carnage on the Western Front, but the Italians and the Austrians fought a desperate war with

A view of the Blindsee where the Fernpass crosses the Lechtal Alps

high casualties and the complete destruction of whole areas such as the plateau of Asiago. Along our route the principal battleground was Monte Pasubio, where there are two war memorials on spectacular sites.

Both sides have romanticized this Alpine war to an astonishing degree, and to this day the *Alpini* are one of the most dashing Italian regiments. If you are interested in the conflict, visit the main museum of the Italian campaign in the fortress of Rovereto, on our route. There you can learn of such peculiarities as the armour worn by some Italian regiments, and the winter quarters hacked out within glaciers (see p. 157).

Look for the Piazza Cesare Battisti in these towns. Cesare Battisti was the great Tyrolese patriot who was shot as a traitor by the Austrians at the Castle of Trent during the First World War. In the struggle for the area's independence he replaced the nineteenth-century patriot Andreas Hofer in the Tyrolese pantheon.

The only really fierce pass on this route is Timmelsjoch, 2509m (8232 feet) above sea level. It is crossed by an Austrian toll road at the border with South Tyrol. All the passes can be crossed by car or bicycle without a detour, though of course walkers can nearly always find alternatives to the motor road on our strip maps. The route has four passes over 1100m (3600 feet), so cycle tourists may find the Amber Route the most satisfying of all our Alpine adventures.

Tyrolean costume from Meran

0   1   **2km**

Mad King Ludwig's Fairy-tale Castle

A short detour to the south-east from Füssen are the castles of Hohenschwangau and Neuschwanstein. Hohenschwangau is a medieval castle, rebuilt in the nineteenth century by King Maximilian II of Bavaria. His son, the mad King Ludwig II, had the castle of Neuschwanstein erected near by on a precipitous rock, high above the plunging ravine of the River Pöllat.

Designed in the Romanesque style, Neuschwanstein as we see it today is like all the fairy-story castles there ever were. It was the joint creation of the king himself and his architects. Ludwig was partly inspired by the work of his protégé, the composer Richard Wagner, and partly by a visit in 1867 to the Wartburg, near Eisenach in Hesse, where he admired the newly restored Minstrels' Hall. The royal apartments of Neuschwanstein on the third floor contain a remarkable sequence of rooms, all richly decorated. These include the Minstrels' Hall, painted with scenes from the Quest for the Holy Grail, and the Throne Room, which is partially Byzantine in inspiration. One room contains Wagner's piano.

The town hall at Füssen

Map:

Brunnen
St. Coloman
Schwangau
Bullachberg
Forggensee 781
Waltenhofen
Alterschrofen
Romanische Strasse
Königsstrasse
Horn
Ehrwang
Achmühle
Kienberg
Alpsee 814
Schönblick
Eschach
Electrizitatswerk
Schwarzenberg
Kropfergtal
Kalwarienberg
Kitzberg 1123
Füssen
Hutlesberg
Ziegebvies
Schwangauer Gitter
Lechfall
Zollamt
Rotwand 1127
Zolhaus
1213
Mittersee
Weißhaus
1102
Bad Faulenbach
Electrizitatswerk
Judenbichl
Obersee
Pinswang
Geplant
Lech
Unterpinswang
Hofs
Platte
Süglberg 824
Musau
Reintal
Ulrichsbrücke Fussen
Landenhof
Stegen
Schotterwerk
Ranzen 100?
314

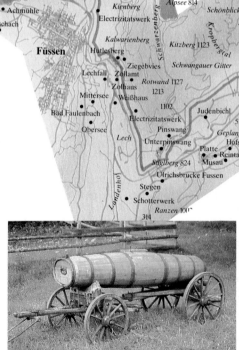

A traditional Bavarian barrel cart

Tyrolean costume from the Ötztal

Füssen: the vertical proportions of an old Bavarian town

The Old Bavarian Town of Füssen

The medieval town of Füssen is full of vitality and interest, as well as being known for its proximity to Ludwig II's castles and the gorge where the River Lech plunges into the Bavarian plain. The main features of historic interest are the castle and the abbey.

The Castle of Füssen guards one of the main German approaches to the Tyrol; the Roman Via Claudia Augusta ran through here on its way south from Augsburg across the Alps. The castle has a splendid Knight's Hall and fifteenth-century religious paintings. The former Abbey of St Magnus was largely rebuilt in the eighteenth century. The church and the state-rooms of the abbey are splendid examples of the Bavarian baroque style, while the chapel of St Anne preserves a Dance of Death painted in about 1600.

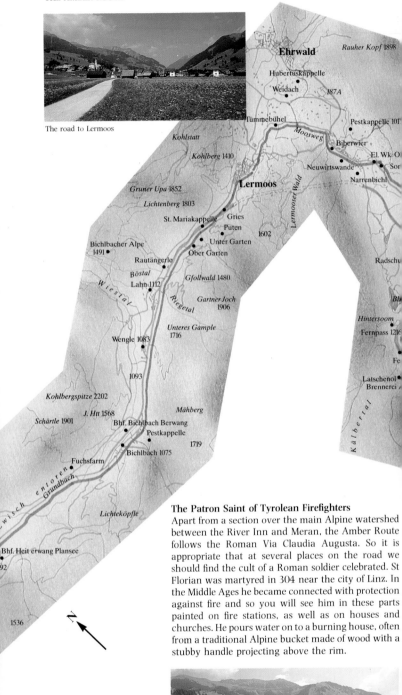

The road to Lermoos

Map labels:

Rauher Kopf 1898
Ehrwald
Hubertuskappelle
Weidach 187A
Tümmebühel
Moosweg
Pestkappelle 101'
Biberwier
Kohlstatt
Kohlberg 1410
El. Wk. O
Neuwirtswande Sor
Narrenbichl
Gruner Upa 1852
Lermoos
Lichtenberg 1803
St. Mariakappelle Gries
Puten
1602
Lermooser Wald
Unter Garten
Bichlbacher Alpe
1491
Ober Garten
Radschu
Rautängerle
Böstal
Lahn 1112
Gfollwald 1480
Wiestal
Riegetal
Gartner Joch
1906
Bl
Hintersoom
Fernpass 1216
Unteres Gample
1716
Wengle 1083
Fe
Latschenol
Brennerei
1093
Kohlbergspitze 2202
J. Htt 1568
Mähberg
Schärtle 1901
Bhf. Bichlbach Berwang
Pestkappelle
1719
Kälbertal
Bichlbach 1075
Fuchsfarm
Grundbach
wisch entoren
Lichteköpfle

The Patron Saint of Tyrolean Firefighters

Apart from a section over the main Alpine watershed between the River Inn and Meran, the Amber Route follows the Roman Via Claudia Augusta. So it is appropriate that at several places on the road we should find the cult of a Roman soldier celebrated. St Florian was martyred in 304 near the city of Linz. In the Middle Ages he became connected with protection against fire and so you will see him in these parts painted on fire stations, as well as on houses and churches. He pours water on to a burning house, often from a traditional Alpine bucket made of wood with a stubby handle projecting above the rim.

Bhf. Heit erwang Plansee
92

1536

A scatter of huts in the fields near Lahn

Smuggling across the Mountains to Bavaria

The Bavarian border lies just 8km (5 miles) north-east of Lermoos, and the area was once a smuggler's paradise. A century ago Baillie Grohman, an Englishman who made his second home in Tyrol, discovered what was going on. In his book *Tyrol and the Tyrolese* (1876) he says that in about 1800,

> . . . smuggling was one of the chief resources for many of the inhabitants of the remote valleys and glens in Tyrol, adjoining either Bavarian or Italian

A view of the Blindsee

St Christopher on
Imst church

boundaries. The Tyrolese smugglers were renowned in those days not only for the bold and cunning manner in which they carried on their dangerous trade – often on an amazingly large scale – but also for the daring courage with which they resisted the armed excisemen. Nowadays the decrease of duty on the two or three articles that were smuggled, such as tobacco and silk into Tyrol, and gunpowder, schnapps and salt out of it, renders smuggling far less remunerative.

A St Florian mural on the fire-station at Tarrenz

Crossing the River Inn

The Alps drain into four seas. The Rhine flows from the Bavarian side into the North Sea; the Rhône drains the western Alps into the Mediterranean; the Po takes everything from south of the main watershed into the Adriatic Sea; while the Inn and lesser tributaries drain the eastern Alps into the Danube and thence to the Black Sea. The Inn is therefore one of the big four Alpine rivers.

We cross it here some 200km (125 miles) below its source in Italy; it is already a substantial stream. We meet the Inn at Karrösten just below Imst and follow the left bank downstream for about 4km (3 miles) to the bridge at Mairhof. Here the Amber Route briefly diverges from the Via Claudia to follow a direct ancient trade road to Meran, while the Roman road detours west over the lower Reschen Pass.

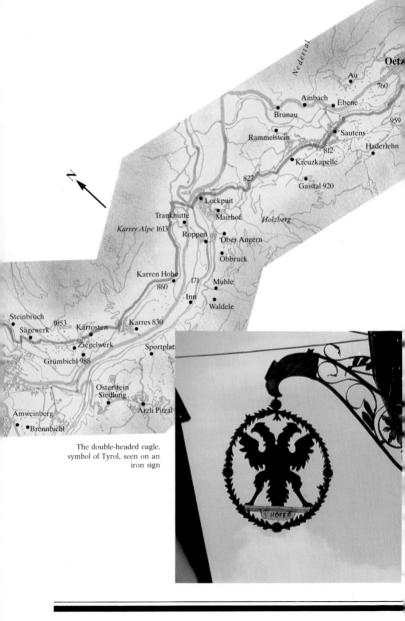

The double-headed eagle, symbol of Tyrol, seen on an iron sign

A typical Tyrolese house, half stone and half wood, seen at Oetz

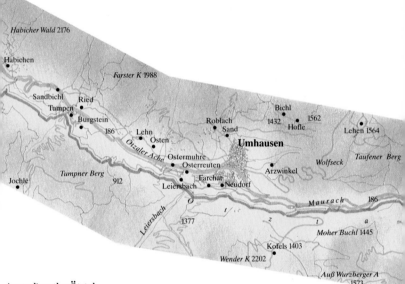

Ascending the Ötztal

After crossing the Inn our route begins to ascend the Ötztal. Since the railway reached Imst in the last century the valley's villages have become summer resorts, health resorts and, lately, ski resorts.

At the mouth of the valley and just opposite Oetz itself lies a jewel of a lake with a curious story. The Piburger See was given in 1282 to the Cistercian monastery of Stams, then a new foundation just down the River Inn. The rule of the house forbade the monks to eat meat, so the fish in this lake formed an important part of their staple diet. For six hundred years their tenants in the lakeside hamlet of Piburg were forbidden to fish. The monastery's long monopoly ended only when tourists discovered the valley. The number of visitors bathing in the beautiful lake so annoyed the monks that they sold it.

The next village, Umhausen, is the oldest in the valley and comparatively unspoilt by ski lifts. The most interesting building is the old Gasthaus Krone (Crown Inn) where customers can see a balconied room on an upper floor still furnished in seventeenth-century style. To learn more of local traditions and crafts, it is worth visiting the Tyrolese Folk Museum at Innsbruck, capital of the region.

Red currants near Moos

Stalking Tyrolean Chamois in the 1870s

This description of hunting chamois in the 1870s comes from the pen of the English sportsman Baillie Grohman in *Tyrol and the Tyrolese* (1876):

The build of the animal exhibits in its construction a wonderful blending of strength and agility. The power of its muscles is rivalled by the extraordinary faculty of balancing the body, of instantly finding, as it were, the centre of gravity. A jump of twenty or even twenty-five feet down a sheer precipice on to a small pinnacle of rock, the point of which is smaller than the palm of a

A seventeenth-century house at Lägenfeld

man's hand, is a fact of constant recurrence in the course of a chamois' flight. . . .

Droves of chamois are not to be met with in all parts of Tyrol, and often and often it has been my fate to be up in the barren, terribly grand recesses of the Tyrolese Alps for days and hardly see a chamois; or, at other times, an unsteady hand at the moment of firing has obliged me to traverse glaciers, snowfields and passes to seek a distant glen or peak where the chamois had not been alarmed by the echoes of my shot.

Frequently two days elapse from the time of leaving the valley before a buck has been sighted and the line of attack

The wide valley of Ötztal above Sölden

resolved upon; and then often, when after endless fatigue and danger the game has been nearly brought within range, the wind may suddenly veer, and a second later a shrill 'phew' of the alarmed chamois tells you that [its] fine scent has frustrated all your designs.

Manifold dangers and adventures of more or less peril, together with the hardships natural to the craft, are the fate of the chamois stalker, till perhaps some day or other he fails to return to his chalet, to his wife and to his little ones. A bullet from the rifle of a hostile keeper, or a treacherous bough, or a loose stone, or a false step pitches him to the foot of a precipice hundreds of feet in height, and years afterwards, perhaps, his bones are found. . . .

Across the Watershed at the Timmelsjoch

From Sölden, the last village in the deep valley of Ötztal, a long-distance footpath (EF5) follows the old track over the Timmelsjoch to St Leonhard in Passeiertal. In 1969 the Austrians completed a toll road across the pass, largely intended for tourist traffic. The summit divides the Adriatic rivers from those flowing into the Black Sea. Along the watershed runs the present Austro-Italian frontier. When Tyrol was united as part of Austria before the First World War the border was 120km (75 miles) away at Lake Garda, but under the Treaty of Versailles in 1919 Italy annexed all of German-speaking Südtirol.

The footpath follows the old road up the Timmelstal

The church at Platt seen from the old road

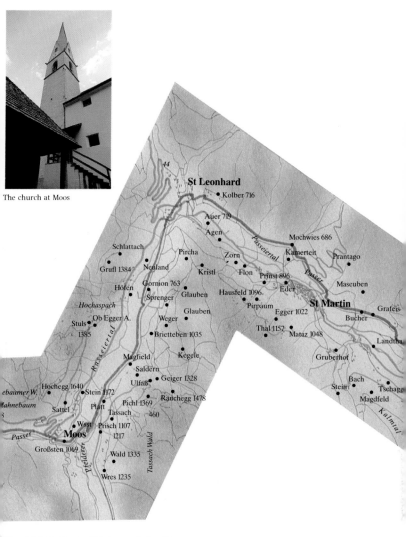

The church at Moos

The Adriatic Ports of Spina and Aquileia

As the Amber Route crosses its highest pass it is timely to recall where the ancient trade was heading. The Veneti and other tribes in the Italian plain kept some of the goods, but much of the trade carried on to the northern Adriatic ports and more distant horizons.

In about 530 BC the Etruscans began to spill over the Apennines into the Po valley. An immediate consequence was the founding of a port to exploit the trade with Greece. Spina, on a lagoon some 80km (50 miles) south of Venice, flourished until about 300 BC. In 1956 part of the city was located by aerial survey: its site is now far inland. The area continues to yield huge quantities of pottery, now to be seen at Ferrara.

Another Adriatic port noted for its connection with the amber trade was Aquileia, founded in 181 BC on a lagoon to the east of Venice. It was once the fourth largest city in Roman Italy, and a place of such importance that the Emperor Augustus met Herod the Great, King of Judea, there in 10 BC. The port declined in the early Middle Ages. A visit today is an evocative experience because of the contrast between the magnificent Roman remains and the present out-of-the-way village of just 3000 people.

Andreas Hofer

Tyrolese Patriot: Andreas Hofer

Andreas Hofer was born in 1767 at Maso della Rena, a mountain village 18km (11 miles) from Meran. He was an innkeeper. He was also a Tyrolese nationalist, staunchly opposed to the occupation of his country.

At the beginning of 1805 Tyrol was under the dominance of the Habsburgs, the ruling family of Austria. But Austria became involved in war against France and its new all-conquering emperor, Napoleon I. In December Napoleon crushed the Austrians at the Battle of Austerlitz, and they sued for peace. Under the terms of the Treaty of Pressburg, signed on Boxing Day, Austria ceded Tyrol to one of Napoleon's allies, Bavaria.

Hofer preferred Austrian rule to that of Bavaria. In 1809 he led a Tyrolese insurrection in support of an attempt by Austria to recover the lands it had lost to

The eponymous castle above Dorf Tirol

Napoleon, and was appointed governor of the Tyrol. Again the Austrians were defeated, and Hofer and his forces were left to carry on their fight alone.

From 1810 to 1813 Tyrol was declared to be part of the Napoleonic kingdom of Italy. Despite some notable victories, Hofer had to retreat with a small band into

Val Passiria. But a traitor was found to betray him, and on 28 January 1810 a French expedition of 1400 infantry, 50 gendarmes and 70 cavalry captured him in a hayloft in the woods at Riffel in the Passirian Alps. He was taken to Mantua, where a tribunal bowed with some reluctance to Napoleon's orders and condemned Hofer to death. He was executed by a firing squad on the bastions of the Porta Ceresa at Mantua.

Hofer's life and exploits became a favourite subject for artists later in the nineteenth century. A splendid monument in his honour can be seen outside the railway station at Meran.

The Castle which gave its name to Tyrol

Castle Tyrol rises on a spectacular site about 3km (2 miles) above Meran. It was from this base in the thirteenth century that the Counts of Tyrol gained control of the whole country, from here across the main Alpine watershed as far as Innsbruck. The fortress passed to the Habsburg dynasty in 1363. Today it is popular with German visitors. There is fine sculpture in the Romanesque doorways of the Knight's Hall and the Chapel.

The path from Meran to Tirol

A view of Brandis from the high road

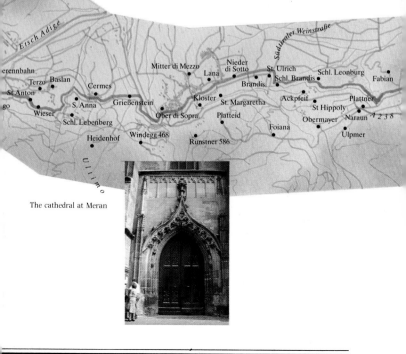

The cathedral at Meran

Bolzano

Bolzano (German Bozen) is the principal town of South Tyrol. It is located at the confluence of the Tálvera and Isarco rivers, which together flow into the Adige about 3km (2 miles) to the south-west, and has been the capital of a province since 1927. During the Middle Ages Bolzano was an important market town, strategically positioned on the route from the north to Venice.

The castle at Prissian is one of many defending the Brenner road

Bolzano cathedral

Bolzano

Po

B.F. Sigmund

Kohl

Riva di Sotto

Schober Brücke

M

Schl. Hochepa

Andrian   Strada del Vino   Brugg

Persdonig   Leo

Steinbruch   St. Vigilius   Aigner

F.sa d'Adige

Burg Wolfsthurm   Reater

Südtiroler Weinstraße   Tratterhof   Gaid

Kofler   Il Castelliere

Nals

Kasatsch   Schwanburg

Ruine Pfefferburg   Payesberg   Sattelhof

Moosbauer   Ob. Wehrburg   Sirmian

Schießstand   Katzenzungen

Vorichi   Prissian

St. Christof   Wehrburg

Fabian   St. Anton   Fahlburg

631

Lattner   Tisens   Zwingenburg

238   Freudenberg

Ulper

Vines growing on traditional wooden poles at Andriano

A German street at Caldaro

An old stone house with a dovecote at Caldaro

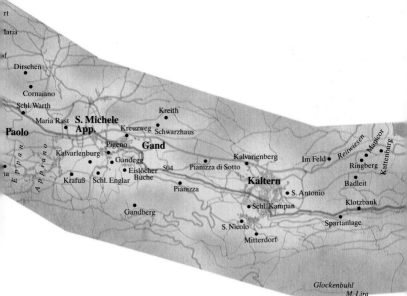

Its control was contested between the Bishops of Trent and Counts of Tyrol until 1276. It passed to the Habsburg family in 1363, and to Bavaria in 1805. From 1810 to 1813 it formed part of the Napoleonic kingdom of Italy, returning to Austrian control until 1918, when it became Italian once more.

The recurrent shift in its fortunes is reflected in the contradictions of its language and culture, with a predominantly Italian-speaking population, but with German Gothic buildings and Tyrolean arcades in the heart of the old town. Visit the Gothic parish church, with its distinctive openwork spire (1501–19) by Johann Lutz. The collections in the Museo Civico include several rooms furnished in the Tyrolese style, with elaborate painted ceramic stoves, and wooden panelled walls. In addition to a number of medieval altarpieces, the museum's art collections contain a portrait of Andreas Hofer, and a fascinating panoramic view of Bolzano in 1790, depicting the ceremonial entrance of Queen Maria Luisa of Spain.

At the sign of the White Horse

A German–Italian Cultural Border

We can be sure that the Roman road, the Via Claudia, followed the right (west) bank of the River Adige past Bolzano because of the succession of Roman place-names on this side of the valley: Prissian, Grissian, Sirmian, Andrian, Missian, Firmiano and Appiano.

The Romans were probably attracted by the sunny and productive slopes, which today are exploited by neatly kept vineyards. The villages on this side of the valley are linked by the Südtiroler Weinstrasse, or South Tyrol Wine Road, which runs all the way down

A typical old farm among the vineyards at Kurtatsch (Cortaccia)

A bronze spout at Magreid

to Trent. Typical of the area is the beautiful farmhouse near Kurtatsch (pictured left), frescoed with lozenges and set among its vines.

The buildings in these pleasing villages have much more in common with northern Europe than with Italy. The finer houses have tall gables with finials and Gothic turrets. The church of SS Quiricus and Julitta at Tramin is a good example of this German flavour: its tall flamboyant Gothic tower is crowned with a thin crocketed spire, while outside a relief of St Christopher displays very Celtic eyes. There is a rare survival at the monastic settlement of St Paul's nearer Bolzano, where no. 16 Via S. Paulo is a complete medieval shopfront with a date-stone inscribed 1575. Beside the carriage entrance is a counter which gives straight on to the street. At Magreid, the last of these Gothic villages, a curiosity is a set of funny peeping people painted on the wall of an old house.

A tombstone at Mezzocorona

A curious peeping head on a house at Magreid

The St Christopher at Tramin

Both the language and the buildings change suddenly from German at Magreid to Italian at Rovere della Luna, the next village. A simpler system of proportions replaces the fussy detail and vertical emphasis of the northern houses, while frescos on the façades give way to a yellow ochre wash. A splendid example of the language boundary can be found on a German map of about 1911, where the next village, Mezzocorona, is called Mezzo Tedesco, meaning Half German, but in a mixture of Italian and German!

Another historic feature of the Adige valley is its strategic importance as the approach to the Brenner Pass. Between Tramin and Meran there are no fewer than twenty-six castles, but many of them in ruins.

A 1917 photograph of the
Tyrolese patriot Cesare Battisti

Tyrolese Patriot: Cesare Battisti

To be a true Tyrolese patriot you have to be captured and shot by your oppressors. Such was the fate of Andreas Hofer, and it was also the destiny of the man who now shares Hofer's mantle.

Cesare Battisti was born in 1875. He was a socialist, idealist, patriot, intellectual and romantic man of action. He was an Austrian subject, but in 1915 he seized the opportunity offered by Italy's entry into the First World War against Germany and Austria to rid Tyrol of the Austrian yoke.

In 1916 Battisti led an attempt to take the Corno at Monte Pasubio, south-east of Trent, but he was captured and imprisoned by the Austrians. (At the huge Castle of Trent it is possible to visit the cells of Battisti and his confederates.)

To a long catalogue of injustice and stupidity in Tyrol the Austrians now added the mistake of making martyrs of these three men. At the castle can also be seen the moat, the so-called Fossa di Martiri where the Austrians shot these patriots as traitors, and the modest monument which marks the site of their death.

Neptune in the main square at Trent

The double-headed eagle of Tyrol seen on a relief at Trent

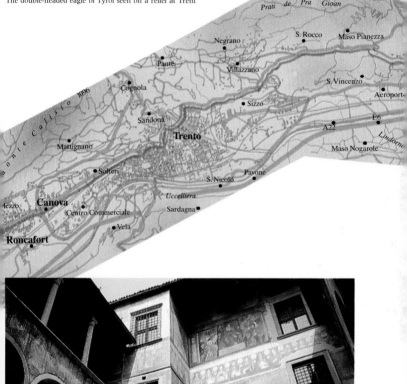

The City of Trent

Trent, capital of its province, was known by the Romans as Tridentum. It was dominated almost continuously by its prince-bishops from the tenth century until 1796. Their residence, the Castello del Buonconsiglio on the east side of the town, played host in the sixteenth century to the Council of Trent (1545–63) which met intermittently to review and reaffirm Roman Catholic dogma during the challenge of the Reformation. In the choir of the church of Sta Maria Maggiore is a group portrait of council members. The enormous castle now houses an archaeological museum and an art gallery.

Castello di Buonconsiglio where the Council of Trent met in 1545–63

The Battle of Monte Pasubio

The following description of high alpine fighting comes from *Scenes from Italy's War* (London, 1919), written by the historian G. M. Trevelyan who commanded a British Red Cross ambulance unit in the Italian Campaign from 1915 to 1918.

> [In March 1918] we shifted ground [from the Asiago plateau], moving our hill stations into the service of the 10th Army Corps at Arsiero, and of the 5th Army Corps in Vallarsa, on the two sides of the Pasubio massif. We now saw for the first time the real high-alpine war, differing as much from the life on the Asiago plateau as from that on the plain of the Piave itself.
>
> Our work lay, of course, at the foot of the *teleferiche*, or aerial railways, which fed the war on those astonishing rock citadels: the sick and wounded came down the wires in

Castel Beseno seen from
the valley at Nomi

> cages, hundreds of feet in the air.
>
> Arsiero, situated at the junction of the Posina and upper Astico torrents, lies at the very foot of Monte Cimone, an acropolis of immense proportions then occupied by the Austrians. They could almost have thrown stones, and they could fire machine guns, into the streets of Arsiero from their perch 3000 feet overhead. The Italian line defending the town hung on to an isolated pinnacle of rock, as grotesque a position as anything depicted in Captain Bairnsfather's Italian tour. . . .

A view of Rovereto

A nineteenth-century view of Rovereto

One day I visited the Pria Fora mountain. The Austrians had stormed it in May 1916 when it was wholly unfortified; but they were not likely to do so again, for its massive rocky summit had now been excavated into a labyrinthine fortress, with four storeys of galleries one above the other, each grinning with cannon and machine guns. There were also mediaeval-looking wooden machines for pouring volleys of rocks down the gullies by which the enemy might attempt to ascend. The artillery pointed out to us similar rock fortresses of the Austrians several miles away. . . .

Monte Pasubio from Vallarsa

Haystack above Recoaro

At our other mountain station, Vallarsa, we lay in Austrian territory, on the north side of the watershed, looking down the vale to Rovereto and Trent. The Pasubio massif, over 7000 feet high, towered above us. On its southern and western faces it presented the most superb range of Dolomite chimneys and pinnacles to the view. Although on each of these horns companies or batteries were hidden away, and, in some, men were burrowing and countermining against each other, and swinging themselves about on ropes to give or take sudden death, the war was here a thing so much smaller than nature that in Vallarsa the whole grim business only set off the mountain glory in which it was framed.

It is possible to climb today among the towering pinnacles of rock to reach two dramatically sited memorials to the fighting on Monte Pasubio. This was one of the major battles in the Italian Campaign where the total casualties on the Italian side alone were 460,000 killed with 947,000 wounded.

At the nearby town of Recoaro Terme and elsewhere along the front books can be bought which

The baroque façade of the church at Matassone

Monte Pasubio from Riva

recount the legend of the mountain regiments, the Italian *Alpini* and the Austrian *Kaiserjäger*, their equipment, songs and exploits. The English literature on this desperate campaign is remarkably thin.

An important inn and the Royal Baths at Recoaro in 1903

Branchi 657
Spanevello
Alpe 657   Sbera
                Ma
Floriani   Ongaro
Pianalto   Pintari
Ceola   **Recoaro**
       609   Siche
      Zulpo   Terme
Povareste 929   Prebianca   Cischele
            Ube Capitello
La Sisilla   Merendaore   Frizzi 611   Bruni
      P.so di Campogrosso
      Cima Campogrosso 1502   Asnicar
Sinello   Malga Campogrosso   1530   Rif. Alla Guardia   Giorgetti
   e di Mezzo 1262   1413   1562   Meso Cason
      T. Lesco di Vallarsa   Maltaure
   P.so Buse Scure 1475   1149   F. le Fastro 842   Parlati 656
alga Siebe 1110   Sella del Rotolon 1523   Facci
      Sentiero Europeo E5

Cima Carega from Ometti

First World War memorial, Recoaro

The Iron Age in Northern Italy

In about 750 BC a revolution occurred in Alpine life: iron technology reached the tribes of the Veneti in north-eastern Italy and the Raeti to the north, whose frontier with the Veneti lay in the fringes of the Alps. The new metal was used for tools and weapons, but bronze and copper continued to be used for personal objects because finer detail could be cast in them.

Two Iron Age invaders also left their mark here. Around 500 BC the Etruscans founded many cities in the Po valley, including Mantua. Then about a century later the Celts struck terror in southern hearts by erupting over the Alps. They conquered Rome in 387 BC, and only the Capitol was held, saved by the cackling of geese in the night.

(*Top*) Objects from an Iron Age tomb: bronze and pottery vessels, dress pins and bronze hand mirrors

(*Bottom*) Iron Age objects from northern Italy

A Palladian temple at Monte Magre in the Veneto

Castelgomberto, a Venetian
villa in the Palladian
style, 1755

Villas of the Veneto

Both the Villa Piovene da Schio at Castelgomberto and
the Villa Bissari Curti at Sovizzo typify the country
houses which are dotted throughout this part of the
Veneto. In late antiquity the landed gentry built
provincial villas, some of which provide foundations
for more recent structures.

These estates, abandoned during the barbarian
invasions, regained their popularity with the Venetian
aristocracy in the sixteenth century. Wealthy Venetians saw such acquisitions as prudent investments,
bulwarks against the risks of trade and fluctuating
exchange rates. Their return to the country represented not only an escape from the humid heat of the
Venetian lagoon in midsummer, but also a real
commitment to agricultural improvement.

The most famous of the architects who designed
these villas is Andrea Palladio (1508–80), noted for his
elegant reinterpretation of the classical style. Born in
Padua, he moved to Vicenza 8km (5 miles) east of
Sovizzo in 1524, where he lived for the rest of his life.
There you can see a good selection of his buildings: the
Basilica, the Palazzo Chiericati housing the Museo
Civico, and the world-famous Villa Rotunda.

A butterfly at Brendola

First World War Aviators on the Alpine Front

The First World War was the proving ground for two entirely new weapons, the tank and the aeroplane. Before the holocaust began none of the participants had given serious thought to the military value of aircraft.

Austria-Hungary, for example, had only thirty-six planes and one airship at the outbreak of hostilities in August 1914, all of them intended for reconnaissance and artillery support duties. When Italy joined the allies in May 1915 its *Corpo Aeronautica Militare* had only eighty-nine planes and three airships, again principally for reconnaissance.

The castle keep dominating Brendola

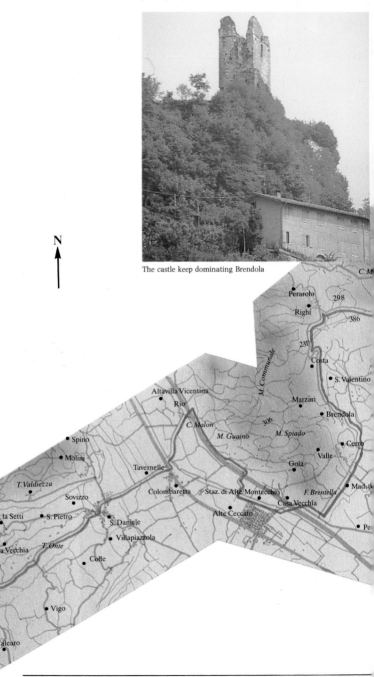

N

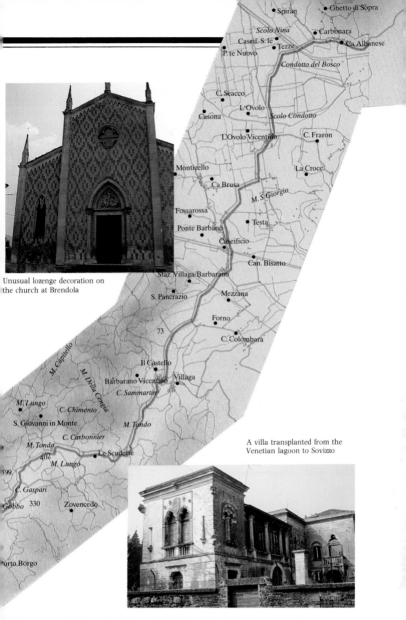

Unusual lozenge decoration on the church at Brendola

A villa transplanted from the Venetian lagoon to Sovizzo

However, within a few days of the invasion of Belgium, Germany was carrying out nuisance raids over Paris with the bird-like Taube monoplanes. The initiative in the air remained with the aggressors for over a year. But by the end of 1915 an element in the growing Allied supremacy in the air was regular Italian bombing raids across the Alps to strike at targets in Austria-Hungary.

Italy was quick to realize the potential for large bombers and night raids: the three-engined Caproni machines were in service by the end of 1915 carrying the then huge load of up to 450kg (1000lb) of bombs over the mountains. Among the Italian aircrews were some of the unsung heroes of the war. In one type of aircraft the gunner stood exposed on the wing protected only by a railing while the machine flew to and fro across the Alps 4500m (15,000 feet) above sea-level!

The allies treated the Austrian aviators as a joke.

Colli Euganei's DOC vineyards

Petrarch's House in the Euganean Hills

The Amber Route follows at its southern end a spur which juts out from the Alps into the Venetian plain. Celebrated for their rolling beauty, the Euganean Hills are covered with forests and productive vineyards. The most romantic of the villages which dot this picturesque landscape is Arquà, renamed Arquà Petrarca in 1868 after its most famous inhabitant.

Francesco Petrarch (1304–74), the Aretine poet best known for his poems to 'Laura', spent the last years of his life here in a house which has been beautifully preserved. He died in the night while working in his study, his head falling forward on to an open book. Near his mausoleum outside the parish church a plaque indicates that the town had already become a focus of literary pilgrimage by 1524. Among the relics in the house is the preserved corpse of the poet's cat.

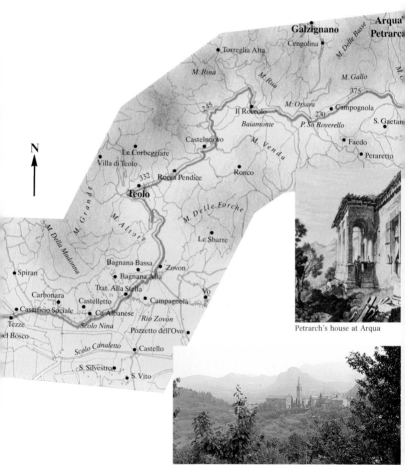

Petrarch's house at Arqua

A distant view of Teolo in the Colli Euganei

Ancient Este and its Archaeological Museum

Este is one of the oldest settlements on the Amber Route, with a history of continuous occupation since the New Stone Age. From the beginning of the eighth century BC the archaeological record becomes steadily richer; the civilization is known as the *Atestino*, from the River Athesis which used to flow through Este. The river, now known as the Adige, today flows 15km (9 miles) further south. The prehistoric collections in the Museo Nazionale Atestino are among the most

Roman milestones and boundary stones in the castle grounds at Este

The south gate at Este

mportant in the whole of Italy. The museum is in part of the castle close to the town centre; it is laid out in chronological order and the history is clear.

Este was a natrual point of exchange between transalpine traders and the people of the plain, and many northern connections are illustrated in the museum. One example is that the same patterns of early iron keys can be seen here and in Austria. Also we can, at last, see examples of Baltic amber. The jewellery on show dates from the thirteenth to the fourth centuries BC. Do not miss the park inside the castle walls, for it contains a collection of more than twenty Roman milestones, which rivals the group in the garden of Klagenfurt Museum in Noricum.

The little city of Este has many other points of interest, including the Romanesque church of S. Martino and an altarpiece by Tiepolo in the cathedral. It is perhaps best known for the noble family of Este, who went on from here to rule the magnificent principality of Ferrara from 1240 to 1598.

THE SWISS ALPS

The Geographical Centre

We have chosen this route through the central Alps in such a way as to demonstrate to the maximum the cultural differences of the people who make up the Swiss nation. While it is true that the people of these valleys share a common way of life with other Alpine inhabitants, the very isolation of the valleys, geographically speaking, has led the communities to develop independently and preserve their own characteristics through the centuries.

Our route passes through the most famous and splendid scenery of the Alps: who has not heard of the heroes (or possibly fools) climbing the north face of the Eiger? But in order to understand the cultural differences that remain in these mountains, we must remember that our admiring response to the scenery is a product of the Romantic movement which began only two centuries ago. Before the advent of the

Romantics it was a very rare traveller indeed who saw the Alps as anything but an ugly and dangerous barrier, to be avoided if possible.

The clearest example of cultural isolation in the Alps is the group of Romansch languages spoken in the Engadine, at the start of our walk in south-east Switzerland. Here, in a remote corner of the old Roman province of Raetia, Latin has been allowed to corrupt itself for two thousand years, more or less free of outside influence.

There are now five distinct dialects of Romansch. If you know Latin and Italian you may be able to read the notices, but to an English ear Romansch sounds like Portuguese spoken with a thick German accent.

It is estimated that only 60,000 Swiss use Romansch dialects as a first language. That is about one-eighth of the British citizens who speak Welsh. The children tend to learn German at school as their second language, although for most of them Italian speakers are only just over the mountain in the canton of Ticino. The probable reason for this choice is that the largest proportion of the Swiss are German speakers.

Nobody outside the canton of Graubünden is required to know Romansch, but you may notice the strenuous efforts that are being made to encourage the use of its dialects within the canton. The people of Graubünden have the reputation of being stubborn and conservative: for example, they kept cars out of their canton until 1923. They certainly need these stalwart qualities if their language is to stay alive in the face of modern communications and the much-resented influx of wealthy German speakers and businesses.

A view in the upper Vorderrhein valley between Somvix and Disentis

The diversity of the Swiss people can be illustrated by the sequence of their first languages along our route through the cantons of Graubünden, Ticino and Valais. The path begins in Val Müstair, in the east, with the main form of Romansch called Ladin, then passes into a cosmopolitan area where German has established a thorough dominance, before reaching the Romansch dialect of Surveltisch in the Vorderrhein valley.

We cross the watershed briefly to dip into a purely Italian town, Airolo, below the St Gotthard Pass before returning to the very source of the Rhône.

Here the German speech begins and flows down the river valley until it suddenly meets the French penetration at a linguistic border drawn with Swiss precision across the valley from one immense field of ice to the other. And so pure French flows out of the Alps with the Rhône into Lac Léman, which you may call Lake Geneva if you like, but not in Lausanne.

The bald language statistics from the most recent Swiss census are: German 74 per cent; French 20 per cent; Italian 5 per cent; Romansch 0.9 per cent. But many urban citizens are truly bilingual, and 15 per cent of the Swiss population are officially 'foreigners', so the figures should be treated with caution.

The desire to tolerate minorities goes deep into the Swiss character, in language as well as religion. For example, in a national referendum held in 1938 the vote was eleven to one in favour of giving Romansch the status of the fourth Swiss national language. In practice this tolerance means little except four languages on the banknotes, because German, French and Italian are the only official languages used by the Federal Government, its publications and staff.

It is open to question whether this desire by German-speaking Swiss not to impose on the minorities is answered by, say, the Italian speakers' willingness not to feel culturally a part of Italy.

The nation's political history is complex. Cantons have been joining the Swiss republic as sovereign states since the first union in 1291, the

League of the Three Forest Cantons (Uri, Schwyz and Unterwalden).

Of the three cantons along our walk Graubünden was a separate self-defence league of twenty-six tiny states, a Switzerland in miniature, until it joined the Swiss republic in 1803. The history of this area is well explained in the Rhätische Museum in Chur, one of the most intelligently arranged and helpful museums in the entire Alps. The Reformation was introduced into the canton in 1521 and was embraced by more than half the population, but a powerful minority adhered to the Roman Catholic faith.

It may save confusion to explain that Grisons, often used in older books, is simply the French name for the canton of Graubünden.

The Italian canton of Ticino was for centuries an occupied territory, a group of districts subject to the original Swiss republic. The French Revolution led to the invasion of Italy by a French army commanded by Napoleon Bonaparte, which gave the districts independence, but in 1803 their people voted to join the Swiss republic as the full canton of Ticino. Today its people are overwhelmingly Roman Catholic and Italian speaking.

The history of Valais is characterized by the strategic position of the Rhône valley at the foot of the St Bernard and Simplon passes, and a series of internecine wars dominated by the splendid and despotic Prince-Bishops of Sion. Batted like a shuttlecock between the Swiss Republic and the French Empire during the Napoleonic wars, Valais finally became the twenty-second canton of the confederation in 1815 as a result of the Treaty of Paris which ended the Napoleonic wars. Despite the efforts of Protestant reformers, the people of Valais remain mostly Roman Catholics.

As far as visible historic buildings along our path are concerned, little remains from the time when Switzerland formed, roughly, the Roman province of Raetia, although Chur (the Roman Curia Raetorum) and Martigny (Octodurum) were towns of local importance in Roman times.

The walk begins at an abbey in Val Müstair founded as a political outpost by the Frankish Emperor Charlemagne. Fortified medieval church sites are a feature of the region. The most striking example is in the Rhône valley, where the fortified cathedral of Valère dominates Sion from its rock. Near the end of the route at St Maurice is the oldest abbey in continuous occupation on the north side of the Alps. Because of its special patronage by the early Burgundian rulers it possesses one of the finest medieval treasuries in Europe.

Most of the surviving historic buildings are nineteenth-century. All along our path can be seen workaday Swiss chalets built in a style and for a purpose which both probably predate the

Romans. The sides of these valleys are so steep that in just a few hours you can walk from a sheltered and sunny vineyard to a desolate landscape of rock and ice. It can seem as if you have travelled thousands of kilometres in a morning, from Burgundy to the Antarctic.

Before the mechanization of agriculture farmers had slowly developed ways of getting the best out of this hard landscape and climate. The Swiss writer Charles Ferdinand Ramuz, regarded as one of the greatest poets of the Vaudois, described how the people of Valais at the turn of the century were trebly fettered to the soil:

> For here they have their house
> amidst the vineyards, another higher
> up in the church village, and a third
> one, still higher, in an Alpine farm.
> In spring, they come down into the
> valley to cut their vine-plants.
> During harvest, they settle in their
> villages where they have their
> homes and spend the winter. For
> hay-making, they go up to their
> Alpine farms.

The route makes a detour out of the Rhône valley so that you can gain a true feeling of this harsh but idyllic way of life. Lötschental is the Shangri-La of the Alps, accessible only through

Linguistic map of Switzerland

a single narrow gorge and completely surrounded by glaciers. Geologists would call it a hanging valley, which is a side valley that enters a main one high up one side because erosion has etched away the larger vale.

On this walk you cross the geographical centre of the Alps at the Furka pass. You see the unforgettable Jungfrau massif and know a dramatic Alpine storm. You meet the rivers Inn, Rhine and Rhône in their youth. Perhaps, best of all, you appreciate the famous Swiss network of footpaths, signposted in hours and marked in colours.

You may even agree that a serious and long-term view can allow a mountain landscape to be both conserved and enjoyed.

House fresco at Sta Maria

Romanesque carving at Müstair

Charlemagne in Val Müstair

Our exploration of the different Swiss people begins in the remote and beautiful Val Müstair. You can see the Romansch dialect in use for mottoes painted on the walls of old buildings throughout the valley. A sample of the language is quoted on page 159; it illustrates the tradition of organ-playing in the local Swiss Reformed churches. Outside influence can be seen in the diagonal cross-bracing of wooden lofts which is typical of Tyrol, and in the high proportion (about 50 per cent) of German names in the graveyards.

At the head of the valley the Benedictine convent dominates the village of Müstair. According to a

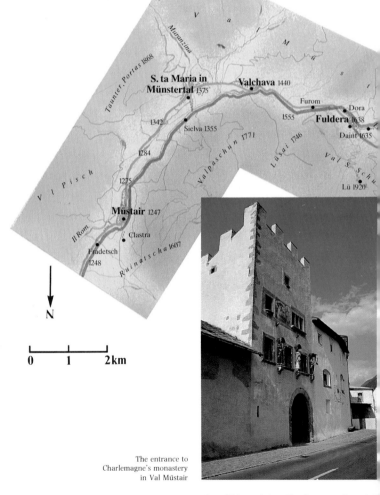

The entrance to
Charlemagne's monastery
in Val Müstair

persistent and credible tradition Charlemagne founded it in about 785 as a monastery and eastern outpost of his revived Roman Empire. Inside the church a unique set of Carolingian wall paintings survives on the north, south and west walls. They were made in about 800, the year that Charlemagne was crowned in Rome. The brighter frescos in the three apses are later Romanesque work, as is the life-size statue of Charlemagne himself on a pillar in front of them.

A Glacier Fortress

This description of the tunnels and fortress within a glacier on the front line at the Ortler Pass also comes from Warner Allen's First World War reminiscences, *Our Italian Front*:

> Trenches are mean and sordid, and have no aesthetic attraction. The ice galleries all formed part of a fairy fortress, an ice palace, which was beautiful beyond human imagining. . . . Out of the burning sun one plunged into the cold stillness of the ice. Outside the snow was

A farm of typically Tyrolean appearance at Sta Maria, Val Müstair

dazzling in its whiteness. Below the light filtered softly through walls of transparent blue. Then as the tunnel burrowed into the heart of the glacier, always inclining upward towards the front line on the peaks above, the light faded away and all was dark except for the flares carried by the guides.

There were long staircases to be climbed, and sometimes to avoid a crevasse there would be a series of deep steps to be descended. Then as a corner was turned, there appeared far ahead a mysterious blue radiance. As one approached it grew stronger and stronger, until the light of the flares seemed dim and yellow.

Half-dazzled, one stepped out of the tunnel on to a crazy narrow bridge of planks. A huge cavern of ice and snow, with the light pouring dazzling white through the mass of snow above and filtering blue through blocks of ice, stretched endlessly on either hand. Beneath, it descended into gulfs of nothingness. A hundred feet overhead, glistening snow crystals, shaped like flowers, formed capitals to pillars of ice.

. . . With regret we tore ourselves away from this fairy throne room and

N

G. Pitzla Scheira 1898

punt la Drossa 1706

Ova dal Fuorn

La Drossa

La Crast' alatscha

1766

1878

Il Fuorn

Spol

Margun Grimmels 1657

s 2130

Muottas Champsech 1975

Ova Spin

Plan Verd 1838

Champatsch 1841

Falcun 200

Champatse

La Serra

V. da Barch

Muni Baselgia 2

An inn sign in Val Müstair

HOTEL CHALAVAINA

Typical engraved house decoration

crossing the bridge went forward along the never-ending tunnel. Again and again we crossed crevasses that were great natural cathedrals, until we came back again to the surface at a point far away up the glacier slope.

. . . There were miles and miles of these tunnels in the ice and their construction never ceased throughout the war. . . One of the most maddening enemies which the Italian's engineers had to contend with was the perpetual movement of the glacier. . . .

The front line of the Ortler pass consisted of a long ice tunnel parallel to the enemy, with openings in its walls for machine guns. Behind the first line of trenches were three wooden huts with their back resting against the naked rock. Here the garrison slept and warmed itself in comparative comfort.

Sample of Romansch Dialect from Graubünden

This is a description of the Organ in the Swiss Reformed Church at Zernez in the Engadine:

Haymaking near Ardez in 1944

Illa baselgia evangelica da Zernez sta il plü vegl orgel d'Engiadina. El porta l'annada dal 1741 ed es gnü construi da Joseph Lochner da Feldkirch. La ditta da construcziun d'orgel Kuhn a Männedorf ha remiss il mecanissem instrumental davo lavur minuziusa i'l stadi uriuntamaing genuin, dovrond il vegl portavent, l'assa uondada dal manual sco eir l'inchaschamaint coluri.

Our dal grand numer da las chonnas da l'orgel sun gnüts applichats trais registers nouvs. Hoz l'orgel as preschainta cun ün cling inrichi da 9 registers cun ün unic manual e cun ün pedal applicà d'ün subbass 16'.

L'intonazuin da l'instrumaint es circa per ün mez tun plü bassa co quai chi'd es il cas normalmaing. L'octava inferiura figürescha i'l manual sco eir i'l pedal sco uschè-dita "octava cuorta" q.v.d. sainza ils tuns Cis, Dis, Fis e Gis. Las tastas sun applichadas in möd seguaint:

DEB
CFGAHc°...

The castle at Zernez

Alpine chapel, Flüelapass

Davos and *The Magic Mountain*

Davos stands amid spectacular scenery at a height of 1560m (5117 feet) above sea-level and has been a highly fashionable health resort since the Victorian period. The scene is described in the 1911 Baedeker guide to Switzerland:

> Davos-Platz, with picturesque houses scattered among the pastures, is a favourite health and sport resort in winter, and attracts visitors in summer also, to the tune of 22,000 visitors annually. In winter the air is generally calm, and the power of the sun is often so great that it is comfortable to sit in the open air even when the thermometer

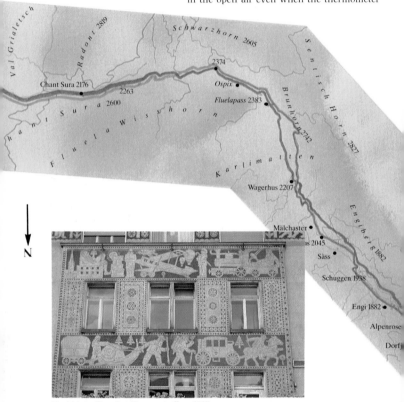

The history of travel on Davos post office, c1920

> is below zero. Skating, tobogganing, curling and ski-ing are actively pursued in winter, and an international skating competition is held in January on the large rink opposite the Kurhaus.

Thomas Mann (1875–1955) used the spa atmosphere of Davos as the setting for his strange novel *The Magic Mountain*, first published in German in 1924. The clinics have all been modernized, if not completely rebuilt, so many times that it is now difficult to see the kind of sanatoria that Mann had in mind, but we did find the Alexanderhaus of 1907 and St Joseph's-Haus on the sunny slope above Davos-Platz. Among the town's other literary friends was the English travel writer John Addington Symonds (1840–93) who lived at Davos for many years and wrote most of his books here. Davos remains very fashionable today, but the town's local character has suffered severely from the wealth of its visitors and invalids.

Crossing the Strela Pass

From Davos our route crosses the Strela Pass by a footpath which climbs nearly 1000m (3250 feet) above the spa. path numbers 3 and 4 ascend from Davos to a hotel at Schatzalp, then the route follows path number 6 via Strela Alp to the Strela Pass itself at 2352m (7717 feet). This is one of only three climbs up foot passes in this book where less energetic tourists can let their pockets rather than their legs take the strain: from Davos-Platz a funicular railway runs up to Schatzalp, and from there a cable car continues up to Strela itself. A track leads down into the valley of Schanfiggtal past three remote and beautiful hamlets, Chüpfen, Schmitten and Dörfli, to reach Langwies, a station on the picturesque *Rätischebahn* (Raetian railway) to Chur.

Sapün Valley from the summit of the Strela pass

Bellflowers, upper Sapün Valley
Marigolds, upper Sapün Valley

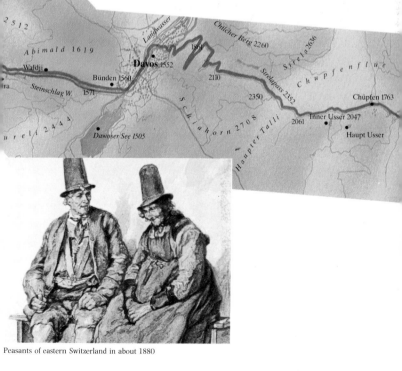

Peasants of eastern Switzerland in about 1880

A house in Dörfli hamlet

Chur, Capital of Canton Graubünden

Chur lies deep in the Alps just below the junction of the twin sources of the River Rhine, called in German *Vorderrhein* and *Hinterrhein*. In linguistic terms the town forms the southern end of the penetration of German speakers into this part of the range, so that our route re-enters a Romansch area when it climbs the Vorderrhein valley after Chur.

Despite being so far into the mountains Chur is easy to reach by following the Rhine valley from Lake Constance. There has been a settlement here since New Stone Age times, five thousand years ago. Some influences came from the south, and the inhabitants were using an Etruscan alphabet before the Romans arrived in 15 BC and called the town Curia Rhaetorum.

The history and traditions of the area are clearly explained here at the Rhätisches Museum which occupies a stately house of 1675 in the old town. One of the best museums in the Alps, it is named after the

enflue 2658

Chüpfen 1763

Haupt Usser   Schmitten   Dörfji 1725

Medergere Alp 2256

Enthalbmald

Rungster Rufi 1337

Langwies 1377

Schluocht   Hof   Grundji

Mattjisch Horn

S. Peter 1274

Peist 1334

Bamald

Fatschaxer Tobel 1600

N

Roman name for the province, Raetia. In the same quarter you can also visit the Bishop's Palace, the Romanesque cathedral of St Maria Himmelfahrt and the early Gothic church of St Lucius, once part of a monastery. The palace and St Lucius form part of the Episcopal Court, which has its own fortifications on the site of the Roman stronghold. In Chur you can see the birthplace of the painter Angelica Kauffmann.

A typical Schanfiggtal farm at Langwies

By Diligence through the Engadine in 1865

Diligence is a Victorian word for what we would call a stage coach. An English observer describes the crepuscular scene at Chur – which he calls Coire – capital of the Engadine, in 1865:

> At dawn everything is still deserted and silent in the streets of Coire. But at the post-office, what a contrast! There is life, agitation and a general hustle and bustle; postilions in bluish-grey coats trimmed with red in their shiny

A Swiss diligence of *c*1880 in the lower Valais

Raetian railway viaduct at Langwies

A house dated 1621 at Castiel   The tower of St Martin at Chur

waterproof hats, are busy polishing the reins, getting their whips ready. . . .

Conductors, men of an Italian type, in their coquettish outfit are busily moving hither and thither, chattering like magpies and piling up letters, packages and bags in their boxes; others in wooden shoes put the last touches to the horses' trappings amid lively shouts of *Hue!* and *Dia!*, resounding loudly in the morning's silence. It is a scene of brisk animation around the four big coaches that are going to start in a moment, either for the Splügen and the Tarasp,

The neat Swiss mask slips, Trin

or else for Disentis and the San Bernadino. . . .

The postilions, perched high on their lofty seats, the reins of their five horses held tightly together, are merely waiting for the signal to start; the *maître de poste*, holding the list of travellers in his hands, with an air of importance, shouts the passengers' names and points out their seats. Amid a tremendous din and commotion, the heavy vehicle rumbles through the streets of old Coire, followed by a concert of barking, howling dogs.

The Baedeker 1911 guide to Switzerland is a little more succinct in its description of the diligence service from Chur:

The handsome Post Office, Graben-Str., 5 min. from the station. The Alpine diligences start hence . . . From Coire to *Arosa*, 18½M., diligence thrice daily in 6¼hrs. (descent 3¾hrs.); fare 7 fr. 50 c. (6 fr. in winter); carriage with one horse 30, with two horses 50 fr. . . . From

N

The Germanic main square at Tamins in the Vorderrhein valley

Coire to *Tiefencastel viâ Churwalden*, 18 M.
Diligence twice daily in $4\frac{3}{4}$ hrs. (7 fr. 25
c., coupé 8 fr. 40 c.); also in summer
twice daily to Lenzerheide in 3 hrs. 10
min. (4 fr. or 5 fr. 50 c.) and once daily
from Lenzerheide to Tiefencastel in $1\frac{1}{4}$ hr.

Two observations can be made. Firstly, both writers assume only one other modern language is known to the English traveller and so Chur is called by its French name, Coire; and secondly, the currency is also French. Strange as it may seem in these days of the 'Gnomes of Zürich', when Baedeker was compiled the Swiss monetary system had been assimilated to that of France since 1851.

Fortified Churches along the Rhine Valley

An unusual feature of the Rhine valley is a string of churches built on fortified hilltops, each with its town clustering on the surrounding slope. Two in particular, at Domat-Ems and Tamins, command spectac-

ular views up and down the River Vorderrhein. Trin church is a third example, first built in about 750. The inhabitants presumably selected the sites as lookouts and places of refuge, perhaps even before the Christian era. Perched between the church and the river at Tamins is Schloss Reichenau, a neo-classical mansion rebuilt in 1819 by Ulrich von Planta, a member of an aristocratic family of Graubünden.

Fortified church, Domat-Ems

The Romanesque portal of Sta Maria Himmelfahrt at Chur

Three peasant women of
Graubünden in c1865

Sumptuary Laws and Rural Costume

Throughout this book we draw attention to the characteristic dress of the country people, but to imagine that this is traditional costume dating from the Middle Ages is to make a fundamental mistake.

All European countries enforced sumptuary laws (literally laws regulating expense) to keep rural costume free from extravagance and indecency. To avoid the squandering of resources on unnecessary luxuries, people were forced to use native instead of imported materials. Nobles were exempted and the bourgeoisie were prepared to pay the fines and cut a dash. The result was that in general the peasants were the only group affected, and this may explain why their dress remained so conservative and colourless until the mid eighteenth century.

To illustrate the restrictions, here are two examples of Swiss sumptuary laws:

1482: Under an income of 1000 guilders, no belt with metal mounts, no silk borders to bodices, no hooks or buckles.

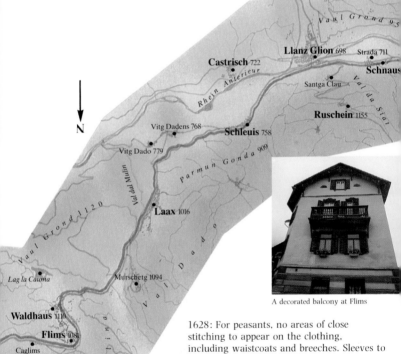

A decorated balcony at Flims

1628: For peasants, no areas of close stitching to appear on the clothing, including waistcoats and breeches. Sleeves to be made of cloth or woollen material according to the class of the wearer. For servants no great, long or thick ruffs. Women forbidden to wear their hair dressed high or their sleeves slashed.

The French Revolution put paid to the Gallic sumptuary laws, and this had an immediate effect on rural costume throughout western Europe. Dress became more elaborate and colourful, quickly developing the local forms now so often considered traditional. Now that the twentieth century has ironed out most of this charm and diversity, you have to attend church in Styria in central Austria to see local costume in unaffected and regular use, or travel to the remoter parts of Romania, Yugoslavia or Sardinia.

The nineteenth-century Savoyard Schlosshotel at Flims

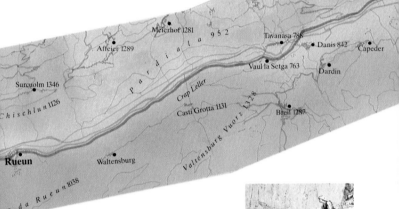

Wali 1052
Meierhof 1281
952
Affeier 1289
Pardiala
Tavanasa 788
Danis 842
Capeder
Vaul la Setga 763
Dardin
Surcuolm 1346
Crap Leller
Chischlun 1126
Casti Grotta 1131
Valtensburg Vuorz 1328
Breil 1287
Rueun
Waltensburg
ns da Rueun 1038

A Swiss peasant saves the trouble of carrying his hay down the mountain by casting it into the abyss (1869)

Local History of the Vorderrhein

Visitors to the resorts of the upper Rhine valley can see many examples of ancient wooden houses and barns in the older village streets or surrounding hamlets. There are three local museums that illustrate the traditional way of life in such houses with a collection of domestic utensils in reconstructed interiors. They are at Laax, Waltensburg/Vuorz and Trun (see map on page 168). The Museum Sursilvan at Trun, founded in 1932, is the largest of the three and occupies a building called the Cuort Ligia Grischa.

A typical Alpine house plan with the stable under the living quarters

Grisons arms, Trun Museum

The Abbey at Disentis

As we climb to the head of the Vorderrhein valley we approach one of the sources of the Rhine. The other main source lies 30km (19 miles) to the south-east in the upper Hinterrhein valley. If the Vorderrhein were a dead-end valley, like Lötschental further along our route, the villages would feel more and more remote as we climbed. But a long-established road leads south from Disentis over the Lucomagno (or Lukmanier) Pass into the valley of the Ticino, a major tributary of the Po. So it is not so surprising to find the village of Disentis dominated by the enormous Benedictine

The upper Vorderrhein valley seen from Somvix

monastery of St Martin.

The abbey was founded here in the eighth century, perhaps with the object of protecting travellers. Remains of the early medieval buildings survive in the present courtyard, where the Klostermuseum displays the history of the monastery. The monks rebuilt the church on a grand scale in 1712 to plans by Brother Caspar Moosbrugger. The interior is of such over-powering baroque splendour that it would be easy to imagine on stepping inside that you were in a capital city like Munich instead of high in the Alps. The earlier high altar dates from 1656 and was brought here from the Gothic church. Disentis is the last large village before the hospice on the Lucomagno Pass.

Choosing a Safe Name

You may well wonder, if you stop at one of the Swiss post offices to buy stamps, why the name of the country appears on those stamps as Helvetia, and not in one of the official languages.

The reason is that when Switzerland introduced adhesive postage stamps in 1850 the authorities could not agree on which language to use, German, French or Italian. So with that gift for compromise which is so necessary in a federation, they decided to use the Latin name Helvetia, which means the land of the Helvetii.

The Helvetii were a Celtic tribe which settled in an area bound by the Jura Mountains, the River Rhine, and Lac Léman about 200 BC. In 58 BC a large number of the Helvetii tried to migrate to Gaul, but were defeated by Julius Caesar. The survivors returned to their homeland.

N

Alp da Laus

Canard

Puxrastg

Rein Anterior   Pardomat 984

Reits 909   Madern

Surrhein 895   Campadials 962

Somvix 1056

Alp Nadels 1481

Rabius 957

Val Rabius

A Crap Ner 1904

Lumneius 844

Zignau

Darvella

Trun 861

Camplium 895

Val Puntegias

antuosch

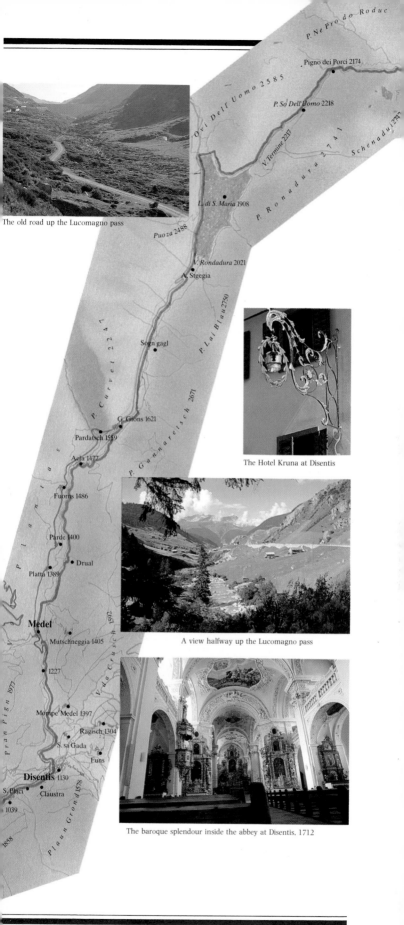

The old road up the Lucomagno pass

The Hotel Kruna at Disentis

A view halfway up the Lucomagno pass

The baroque splendour inside the abbey at Disentis, 1712

Monkshood, Lucomagno pass

Military Ranges at the St Gotthard Pass

The Swiss Army maintains a serious and permanent presence at the St Gotthard Pass, believing that any invader would be trapped at this 'crossroads of Switzerland' and destroyed. Military exercises take place on different ranges surrounding the hospice each day (and night) and intending walkers should consult the army's information board at the lakeside outside the hospice to see whether their chosen areas will be open next day.

Do not be tempted to save a day by crossing a live range: the footpath to Gatscholalücke, though beautiful, is littered with shrapnel, bullets and spent

The deserted village of Valle from Piora

St Gotthard railway tunnel: the monument to the workers who died

rockets. It is best instead to do a circular tour if the path is closed, or to visit the National Museum of the S Gotthard by the hospice, with its simplistic display and propaganda for the military presence around the pass.

Italian Switzerland

Between the Lucomagno and the St Gotthard passes our route goes through the Italian canton of Ticino. The introduction to 'The Swiss Alps' relates how it came to be a part of Switzerland although projecting into Italy as far as Lugano. The language boundary is at the Lucomagno Pass. Although the first Italian signs appear in shops in Disentis, Romansch continues right up to the pass.

In Airolo take note of the thoroughly Italian appearance of the town. Not just the language, but the way the houses are built and the kind of goods people sell here, remind you that this is a valley which faces south. Airolo was almost totally destroyed by fire in 1877. Not surprisingly, one of the few survivals was

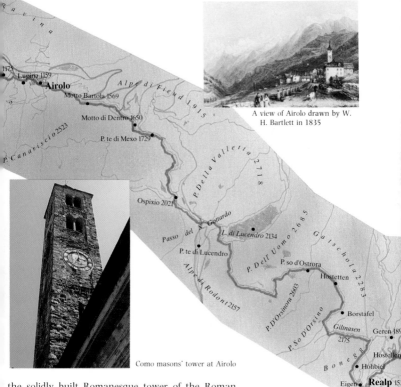

A view of Airolo drawn by W. H. Bartlett in 1835

Como masons' tower at Airolo

the solidly built Romanesque tower of the Roman Catholic parish church of SS Nazario e Celso at the foot of the steep St Gotthard pass: perhaps the Como masons built it. This road was first opened to traffic in the thirteenth century when the hospice was built at the top, although the oldest buildings there now are nineteenth-century.

In the forecourt of Airolo railway station is an impressive memorial to the workers who died during the building of the St Gotthard tunnel, constructed in 1872–82 and only the second rail tunnel to pierce the Alps. Among the victims was the chief engineer, Louis Favre of Genoa, who died of overwork in 1879. The monument's bronze bas-relief shows the Italian workers bringing one of their stricken comrades out of the workings on a stretcher. The sculptor was Vincenzo Vela (1822–91), who came from the southern end of the canton of Ticino. He lived in a house which is now a museum at Ligornetto, a small town on our route 'The Italian Alps and Lakes'.

At the Centre of the Alps

The Furka Pass lies more or less at the geographical centre of the Alps. Halfway across and halfway along the chain, it stands on the triple watershed between the mighty Rhône, those rivers which eventually combine in the Rhine, and tributaries of the Ticino. So from this awesome region of the mountains water flows to the western Mediterranean, the North Sea and the Adriatic. The ridge between Airolo and Furka forms another language boundary where Italian is left behind and German begins.

Just below the Furka we suddenly come across the end of the Rhône glacier, whose slow retreat is watched by the aptly named Hotel Belvedere.

The Rhône glacier: note the figures
standing below it

Victorian Mountaineers in the Alps

A former honorary secretary of the Alpine Club of Great Britain, Edward Pyatt, has described the exclusive nature of the sport in the nineteenth century in his book *The Passage of the Alps*:

> Victorian mountaineers were drawn largely from the professional classes, having enough leisure time to indulge their sport and enough money to smooth the path to success in it. Normal as they then seemed, they were, judged by present-day standards, to some degree snobbish.
>
> In the early days local men were recruited to carry their baggage and help with the hard work; later, as their experience grew, these same locals served to point the way, to guide, where others had gone before. In due course some guides became very good indeed; leading a strenuous outdoor life, they were

Typical wooden houses at Ulrichen in the upper Rhône valley

Oberwald church with a typical onion dome

Traditional fish-scales. Oberwald

The infant Rhône seen from the Hotel Belvedere at the glacier

usually fit and strong, while they developed the judgment to handle awkward situations in terrain and weather.

Some combinations of leading guides and amateurs became quite famous. On the other hand, some guides were almost completely incompetent, and there were several instances where amateurs had to lead their guides in more difficult places. It was not always possible to secure the services of the paragon, and the less favoured had perforce to put up with the rest.

Divided by Religion

The Reformation was introduced into Switzerland by the priest Huldrich Zwingli, who was appointed rector at the Great Minster of Zurich in 1519. Zwingli's preaching was so persuasive that by 1525 the city authorities had accepted the Reformation, closed the monasteries, and allowed priests to marry.

The urban cantons followed Zurich and accepted the teachings of the Protestant reformers, but the rural cantons of Lucerne, Schwyz, Unterwalden, Uri and Zug remained staunchly Roman Catholic.

Civil war followed, and in the Battle of Kappel in

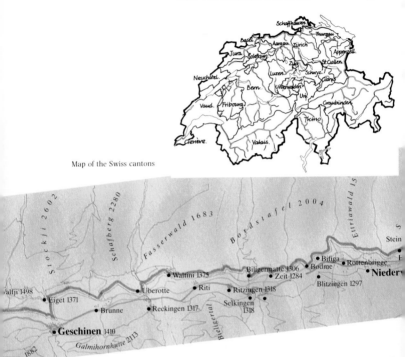

Map of the Swiss cantons

1531 the Protestant cantons were defeated. Zwingli, who was serving as army chaplain, was killed. The two sides then agreed to differ, but not for the first time religion proved to be a divisive force, and for the next three hundred years the cantons were divided, politically as well as in religion.

Ernen: panorama of a typical Walser village

A Typical Walser Village

The village of Ernen, once the principal settlement of the Goms (upper Rhône) valley, is spread out over the slopes of the hillside, its buildings interspersed with intensively cultivated market gardens. German (*Schweizer Deutsch*) is spoken here with quite a different accent from the Romansch/German speaking towns such as Trun, visited earlier on this route.

Many of the picturesque part-wooden buildings were built between the fifteenth and the eighteenth centuries. As at Münster, the upper storeys of the houses and barns are made of thick wooden planks, their joists locked externally by vertical pins running down the middle of each wall. In Ernen, many of the wooden buildings have facings of 'fish-scale' shingles.

The most richly decorated buildings are in the village square, including the Zendenrathaus of 1750–62, with murals on one façade by Henri Boissanas (1953), who also did the paintings on the façade of the school house (1943). The legend of

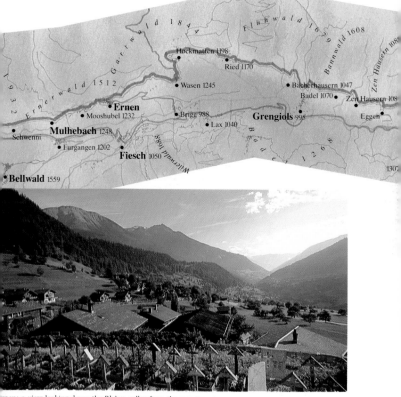

Ernen: a view looking down the Rhône valley from the cemetery

William Tell is depicted on the ground-floor walls of the aptly named Tellenhaus, which stands next door to a wooden storehouse. Visit also the Roman Catholic parish church of St Georg, built in 1510–18 by Ulrich Ruffiner, replacing an eleventh-century church with three apses. The present building consists of a nave and a polygonal late Gothic choir, with a rib-vaulted roof. Its lavish furnishings are noteworthy, including the rococo high altar of 1761 by Plascy Schmidt, and the carved choir stalls of 1666 by H. Siegen and G. Natig. On the north wall of the nave are fragments of a cycle of murals depicting the Apocalypse.

The devil at Naters church

Brig and the Stockalper Palace

Before the tentacles of railway had reached into every Swiss valley, Brig was a centre for diligence (stage coach) travel. The three main crossings were over the Furka, the Grimsel (branching north from the Rhône at Oberwald) and the Simplon passes. C. B. Black's nineteenth-century guide to Switzerland tells us that in about 1875 the 91km (57 mile) journey to Andermatt across the Furka took the diligence twelve and a half hours at a fare of eighteen francs.

Above all Brig is important as the terminus for the Simplon Pass over the main watershed into Italy. After the French victory at the Battle of Marengo in 1800 Napoleon's engineers built a new military road, fit for the passage of artillery, across the pass, taking five years to complete it. Between 1898 and 1906 the Simplon railway tunnel was constructed. At 19½km

Brig: onion domes on the Stockalper Palace

(12¼ miles) it was then the longest rail tunnel in the world.

Much earlier Kaspar Stockalper (1609–91) had dominated the trade over the Simplon Pass, which he protected by a guard of seventy men. His family were traditionally guardians of the Simplon defile but the enterprising Stockalper went much further, making a huge fortune as an international trader in monopolies such as salt. On the proceeds he ornamented his home town with the finest baroque residence in Switzerland. The principal part is the arcaded Stockalper Palace built around a spacious courtyard in 1658–78. Its three tall towers crowned by gilded onion domes form the principal landmark in Brig to this day. The palace is linked by a covered bridge to the earlier family home Peter Stockalper's House of 1535, while opposite the palace Fernanda von Stockalper erected another

Romanesque tower at Naters

Rathaus Junkerhof, Naters

The town of Visp as seen by S. Prout in 1829

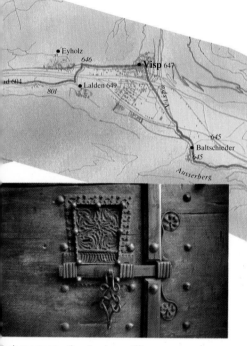

Lock on a seventeenth-century house at Visp

house in 1727, distinguished by a prominent coat of arms facing the street. Inside the palace is the local history museum for Brig, which was the capital of the region in the sixteenth century.

The main religious interest lies in two churches outside the town. The bridge across the Rhône which gives its name to Brig takes us to Naters, once the property of the Prince-Bishop of Sion. There, amid an interesting group of buildings of the fifteenth to seventeenth centuries, stands the Roman Catholic parish church of St Mauritius. A splendid Romanesque bell tower survives from the original foundation, while the nave and its furnishings are baroque.

Soon after Brig our route passes the rich pilgrimage church of Glis, reputedly founded in 615. The late Gothic nave contains fine flamboyant vaulting and much peculiar carving, including an unusual rose window. The eight-stage Romanesque bell tower was rebuilt in 1968. Glis, like all the churches in this valley, has a statue of the martial St George.

Alpine Life in an Isolated Valley

For centuries Lötschental (-*tal* means valley) was at the end of the world, under snow for nine months of the year and accessible only with difficulty by two mule tracks. Its people developed a self-sufficient life ruled by the Alpine climate and untouched by the motor car until 1950. Our route makes a detour to explore the way people adapted to living there.

Lötschental is a hanging valley whose floor lies at a height of about 1340m (4400 feet) above sea-level. Its mouth has been cut off by the Rhône glacier, leaving a

The entrance to Lötschental with a storm brewing

steep drop of 710m (2330 feet) down a narrow gorge to the floor of the Rhône valley. Before the railway tunnel between Goppenstein and Kandersteg was opened in 1913 everything moved on foot or the back of a mule, taking three hours down the defile to reach Steg on the Rhône. The valley is completely surrounded by ice, and the only other way out crosses a glacier at the Lötschen Pass to Kandersteg in seven hours. Under these conditions it is only since 1945 that self-sustaining activities have been eroded by an economy linked to the outside world.

More than a century ago interest stirred in the folk

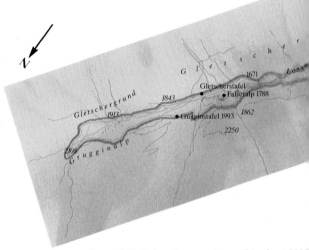

culture of this isolated community, and in about 1910 the painter Albert Nyfeler began photographing the peasants at work on the land and in the home. He used these photographs to help in his own art.

The basis of life in the valley was cattle breeding and dairy farming, combined with growing the few crops which can withstand the harsh mountain climate, principally barley, rye and potatoes. The highest

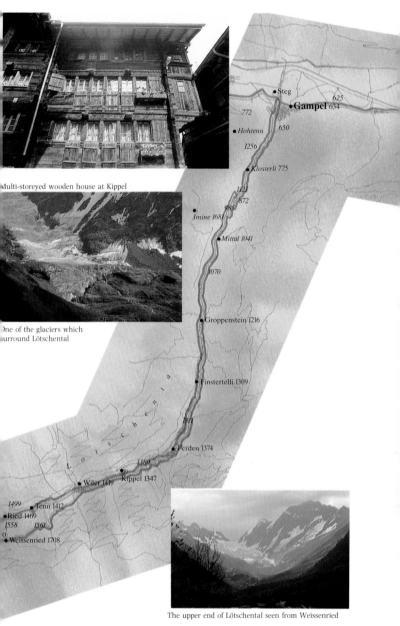

Multi-storeyed wooden house at Kippel

One of the glaciers which surround Lötschental

Steg
Gampel 634
625
772
650
Hohtenn
1256
Klosterli 775
1121
872
985
Imine 1681
Mittal 1041
1070
Groppenstein 1216
Finstertelli 1309
1811
Ferden 1374
1380
Wiler 1419
Kippel 1347
1499
Tenn 1412
Ried 1469
1558
1561
Weissenried 1708

L ö t s c h e n t a l

The upper end of Lötschental seen from Weissenried

arable farming today is an area of barley growing on a south slope at a height of 1750m (5740 feet). Lacking outside help, the people taught themselves many trades, often making their own tools and co-operating to build houses and stables. But in the Alps the land is subject to active erosion, so often all this work would be in vain as avalanches, mountain torrents or rock falls swept down to destroy barns or fields of crops.

Many years of study and collecting show their results in the Lötschentaler Museum in the village of Kippel near the lower end of the valley. Its exhibits evoke the life and labour of the past and how they have changed this century, while its booklets give far more detail than our space allows.

Leuk and the Language Boundary

The small and ancient town of Leuk stands in a fortified position at a constriction in the Rhône valley. Its two castles overlook a classic lesson in geology: the Illgraben torrent's cone of debris, $3\frac{1}{2}$km (2 miles) across. Leuk belonged to the important abbey at St Maurice in 515, and from 1138 to the Prince-Bishops of Sion. Our route passes both these places.

The names of Leuk's castles reflect the dominance of Sion. The Château des Vidames, now the town hall, belonged to the *vidames*, the secular deputies of the French bishops before the Revolution. Rebuilt in the 1540s, it is a gaunt square tower with stepped gables and pretty corner turrets. Immediately to the west stands the Bishop's Palace, rebuilt many times since its first mention in 1254. A beautiful Romanesque bell tower survives from the Roman Catholic parish church of St Stephen. The late Gothic nave was rebuilt from 1497 with flamboyant vaulting. In 1982 two fine medieval statues of the Pietà and St Michael were found here.

After the town our route makes a picturesque circuit round the Dala Gorges. Notice that pasture

The church in a fortified position at Raron

and wooden buildings disappear at this point in the valley, with the exception of just a few half-stone, half-wooden barns in isolated hamlets.

Leuk is one of the last German-speaking places on this route. The linguistic border is a line across the Rhône valley between Salgesch, where we see the last Gothic inscription, and the French town of Sierre. What is surprising here is that the predominant language should change so suddenly when there is no natural barrier between the two communities.

Taking the Waters at Leukerbad

The spa of Leukerbad occupies a magnificent position above Leuk. Sited at the top of a south-facing slope of debris and with its back to precipitous cliffs, it commands a panoramic view of the Rhône and the Pennine Alps from a position 780m (2560 feet) above the valley floor. C. B. Black's guide to Switzerland tells us that by about 1875 seven principal hotels catered for visitors, who came up by diligence from the railway terminus at Leuk in two and a half hours. The fashionable season lasted from May to October.

The waters of the twenty-three thermal springs are full of lime and were recommended for skin diseases, rheumatism and scrofula. In the common bath, comments the Baedeker of 1911, 'the animated conversation of the patients is chiefly in French. Small tables or trays float on the water, bearing cups of coffee, newspapers, books, etc.' The hottest spring is that of St Laurence at a temperature of 52°C (126°F).

The two castles at Leuk

The Rhône and the path before Leuk

medieval house in Salgesch

A house in Salgesch, the last German village

Sierre: the First French Town

Flanked by vineyards and orchards, the sunny town of Sierre is built on the site of a prehistoric landslide. The town and its fortifications originally lay to the south on four hills, each dominated by a château. In the Middle Ages the town was subject to the bishops of Sitten, being administered by vidames and later by castellans. Several of its châteaux, including the Château des Vidames, the Hôtel Château-Bellevue and

Hotel de Ville, Sierre, the first French town

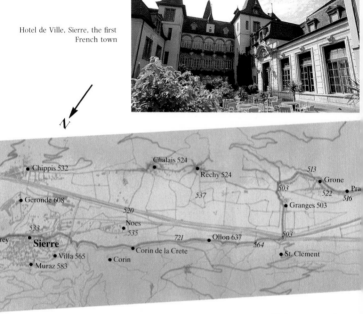

the Château de Chastonay, recall this association.

The Roman Catholic parish church of Ste-Cathèrine, in the Rue du Bourg, dates from 1649. The single-aisled building, built in the baroque style, contains stained glass by Edmond Bille (1924) and Paul Monnier (1946).

One of Sion's magnificent prince-bishops

Sign on the Hotel Poste at Sierre

Sion and its Prince-Bishops

Sion (Sitten in German) is one of many strategic sites along the Rhône valley, and it came to dominate the whole of Valais from its twin citadels overlooking the river. There were probably Celtic settlements on both these rocks. On the height to the north are the ruins of the episcopal castle of Tourbillon, built in 1294 and burned down in 1788. On the slightly lower hill to the south, once the site of a Roman fort, is the castle of Valère. This complex fortress includes the collegiate church of Notre-Dame, which contains the oldest playable organ in the world (c1350; painted doors 1435), on which every August a festival of early organ music is performed. The impressive church has a Romanesque choir and early Gothic nave, separated by a thirteenth-century rood screen. Many wall paintings survive.

The residential part of the fortress houses the Musée de Valère. At the foot of the Valère hill lies the old walled city. Notable buildings include the cathedral, Notre-Dame du Glarier, which was rebuilt after a fire in the fifteenth century, the Supersaxo Mansion (1505), and the Town Hall (1657–65) which has an astronomical clock dated 1667 on its façade. The archaeological and fine arts museums explain the story of the whole canton of Valais.

Tower of Notre Dame, Sion

The history of Sion is one of a struggle for power and rights between the citizens, the glorious and despotic prince-bishops on Tourbillon and the Chapter of Sion

The Bishop's Castle at Sion, seen from the nearby hill of Valère

on Valère. The bishopric was founded in the fourth century, and Sion was made the capital of Valais two hundred years later. In 888 Valais became part of the kingdom of Burgundy. In 999 the last Burgundian king, Rudolf III, gave Valais to the church of Sion, making the bishop a sovereign prince with full royal prerogatives.

The prince-bishops were strong rulers, often at war with the dukes of Savoy, but the people gradually whittled away their privileges. A patriotic uprising in 1630 compelled the prince-bishop to give up his territorial claims. Napoleon I's annexation of Valais finally put an end to the temporal power of the bishops.

A Romanesque Priory in the Vineyards

A few minutes' walk from Chamosan towards the river brings you to the village of St-Pierre-de-Clages. You will have noticed in Valais how often only the Romanesque bell tower survives from earlier buildings. Here the whole church as well as the tower is early twelfth-century. The first documentary reference is to the Benedictine priory of St Pierre in 1153; the priory was suppressed in 1580. The most interesting view is at the east end, where you can see the pilasters decorating the outside of the three apses. Over the crossing rises a two-stage octagonal tower with a pyramid cap. The west end is more rugged and this character continues into the dark nave. The three-storey range of priory buildings on the south side of the church is now put to agricultural use.

Romanesque church door handles, St-Pierre-de-Clages

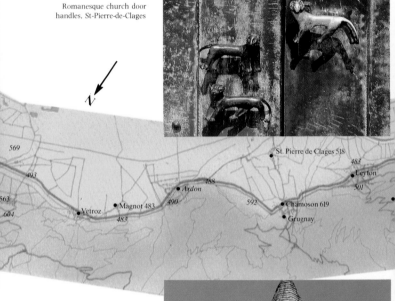

The Romanesque tower on the monastery at St-Pierre-de-Clages

Saillon: a Fortified Town

The Rhône valley abounds in castles and ancient fortified sites: Visp, Leuk, Salgesch, Sierre, Granges, Sion, Saxon, Martigny, St Maurice, Bex, Aigle and Chillon are just a few we pass on our way downstream. The castle at Saillon fell into comparative obscurity when the Rhine changed course and the place lost its strategic position as a bridgehead. Saillon was once a highly important trading station and fortress. The main road ran the length of the town and was perhaps even diverted through the town to control the traffic.

The castle is first mentioned as belonging to the prince-bishop of Sion in 1052 but later was under the control of the Savoyards. Peter II of Savoy built the castle and the strong fortifications around the town in

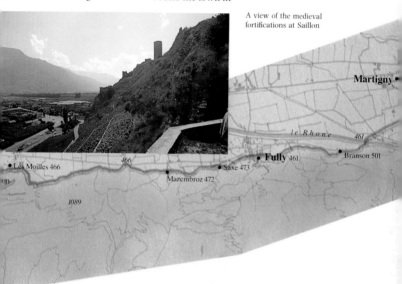

A view of the medieval fortifications at Saillon

1257–58. Pierre Meinier added a keep on top of the outcrop in 1260–61. The town walls are strengthened by a series of projecting semicircular towers and they enclose the whole eastern side of the hill. The castle itself was largely destroyed in 1475 when the Savoyards were driven out.

The town now occupies only about half the area inside the walls. Due to the decline in Saillon's importance compared with that of other towns in the valley, the streets preserve the distinctive atmosphere of the thirteenth-century foundation to a remarkable extent. At the parish church of St Laurent only the Romanesque belfry survives from that time. A climb up the hill is rewarding for the view from the ramparts of the medieval street plan and the grey roofs.

The Rhône valley seen from the fortified town of Saillon

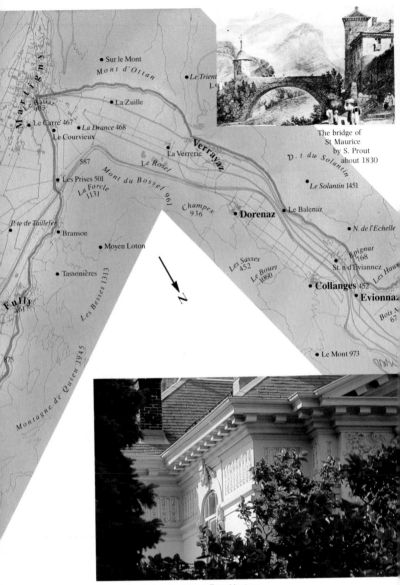

The bridge of
St Maurice
by S. Prout
about 1830

Glimpse of a nineteenth-century villa at Martigny

Junction for the Great St Bernard

Martigny, the site of a Celtic *oppidum* (town centre) in 57 BC and later the Roman imperial market town of Octodurum, is an important station on the road to the Great St Bernard Pass. Sited at the confluence of the Rhône with the River Drance, it also receives traffic from Chamonix and the Forclaz Pass.

Dominating Martigny is the tower of La Bâtiaz, one of the most impressive medieval buildings in the Valais, with a circular keep. It was commissioned by Peter II of Savoy, ruler of the castle from 1260 to 1268. Visitors to Martigny have included Napoleon I, who stayed at the provost's house behind the parish church of Notre-Dame-des-Champs. Johann von Goethe and Alexandre Dumas were guests at La Grande Maison, a former inn at Place Centrale No. 7. The Fondation Pierre Gianadda houses a Gallo-Roman museum and a collection of vintage cars.

The Medieval Treasury of St Maurice

The town of St Maurice was once the Celtic settlement of Agaunum and later became an important Roman military base. Now it contains the oldest abbey with a continuous existence north of the Alps.

The saint after whom the town is named, Maurice (Latin Mauritius), was a *primericius* or Roman cavalry commander. Legend has it that he was slaughtered by command of the Emperor Maximian (*c*302) for being a Christian and refusing to acknowledge the Roman gods. The monastery named after him was founded in 515 by Sigismond, King of Burgundy, who adopted the Byzantine tradition of sleepless praise, creating a rota of monks who sang psalms over the saint's tomb. Regular monastic life lapsed in the tenth century, but was revitalized with the establishment of the canons regular of St Maurice in 1128.

The abbey's treasury contains a number of remarkable objects, including a sardonyx chalice consisting of a carved late Roman cup set in seventh-century Merovingian cloisonné enamel mounts. The

The château at Aigle stands among its own vineyards

Casket of Teuderic is covered with a network of gold filigree lines (*cloisons*) set with classical intaglio gems and a central cameo. On the back the incised inscription reads (in translation): 'Teuderic the Presbyter ordered this to be made in honour of St Maurice. Amen. Nordoalaus and Rihlindis got it made. Undiho and Ello made it.' It is thought that the casket was made in the sixth century for St Theudericus, abbot of Vianne. The craftsmen were Burgundian and the inscription is an exceptionally early reference to named makers.

The treasury also possesses a golden jug, said to be the gift of the Emperor Charlemagne, inset with superb enamel panels of Persian design and possibly Byzantine workmanship, representing lions and griffins. A number of shrines include the head reliquary of St Candidus, a fine silver bust containing the martyr's skull, and the shrines of St Maurice and St Sigismund, both in the form of chests with pitched roofs.

Aigle
657
Grande Eau
Vers Pausa
Les Pesses 800
Les Rennauds
Drapel 671
Champillon 936
Versvey 382
Vers Morey 521
Les Lavanches 669
Vers Cort 754
Chambon
Le Clos
Corbeyrier 920
Roche 382
1039
Sauquenil 346
La Sarse 1626
Eau Froide
1085
Rennaz
Le Chatelet
1266
600
375
Carriere d'Arvel 613
1466
Villeneuve
Le Chatelard 439
Lac
Grandchamp
Chat. de C
Doran
Territet 58
La Veraye

The colourful street scene in Villeneuve

The Château of Chillon in Lac Léman (Lake Geneva)

Lord Byron and the Castle of Chillon

On a rocky islet at the eastern end of Lac Léman is the Castle of Chillon, immortalized by Lord Byron in his poem *The Prisoner of Chillon*. Its hero is François de Bonivard, a prior who was imprisoned at Chillon from 1530 to 1536 for supporting the citizens of Geneva against the tyranny of Duke Charles III of Savoy. When Byron wrote the poem in 1817 – at the Anchor Inn at Ouchy on the shore of Lac Léman while detained by bad weather – he knew little of Bonivard's story, and afterwards said he would have tried to portray his courage more fittingly. Byron later prefixed his poem with a sonnet containing these lines:

> Chillon! thy prison is a holy place,
>   And thy sad floor an altar – for 'twas trod,
> Until his very steps have left a trace
>   Worn, as if thy cold pavement were a sod,
> By Bonnivard! May none those marks efface!
>   For they appeal from tyranny to God.

After his release Bonivard became a Protestant, and was married four times. He died in 1570.

The End of the Pathway

This, the longest of our ancient pathways, has taken us through remote and peaceful valleys – Müstair and the Engadine – the tight knot of awesome mountains around the Furka Pass, and finally into the long valley of the River Rhône.

There can be few places in the Alps which have seen so many battles as that valley, or watched so many armies marching through on their way to war. So it is appropriate that our journey ends amid castles, not only the grim walls of Chillon, but Bex on the banks of the River Avançon, founded in the twelfth century, and the turreted castle of Aigle, still dominating the slopes of well-ordered and productive vineyards that surround it.

BIBLIOGRAPHY

General Reading on the Alps
ALLEN, Warner, Our Italian Front, painted by Martin Hardie (London, 1920)
BROCKEDON, William, Illustrations of Passes of the Alps, 2 vols (London, 1828)
FREESTON, C. L., Cycling in the Alps (London, 1900)
PAULI, Ludwig, The Alps: Archaeology and Early History (Munich, 1981; Bologna, 1983; London, 1984)
PYATT, Edward, The Passage of the Alps (London, 1984)
TREVELYAN, G. M., Scenes from Italy's War (London, 1919)
VIVIAN, Herbert, Italy at War (London, 1917)

The Drove Roads of Provence
ALLEN, Percy, Impressions of Provence (London, 1910)
BRUNHES DELAMERE, Mariel J., Techniques de Production: l'élevage (Paris, 1975)
CHARLES-ROUX, J., Le Costume en Provence (Paris, 1909)
CHASSILLAN, Henri, La Transhumance: temoinage vécu (Raphèle-lès-Arles, 1985)
JOHNSON, Clifton, Along French Byways (London, 1900)
MAURON, Marie, Au Pays des Bergers, photographs by René Mannent (Paris, 1981)
MAURON, Marie, La Transhumance du Pays d'Arles aux Grandes Alpes (Paris, 1959)
PROAL, Maurice & MARTIN CHARPENAL, Pierre, L'Empire des Barcellonnettes au Mexique (Paris, 1986)

The Waldensians' Glorious Return
ARNAUD, Henri, The Glorious Recovery by the Vaudois of their Valleys, Hugh Dyke Acland (ed.) (London, 1827)
GILLY, Canon W. S., Narrative of an Excursion to the Mountains of Piedmont (London, 1824)
GILLY, Canon W. S., Waldensian Researches during a Second Visit (London, 1831)
GONNET, Jean & MOLNÁR, Amedeo, Les Vaudois au Môyen Age (Turin, 1974)
MEILLE, J. P., General Beckwith: His Life and Labour amongst the Waldensians of Piedmont (London, 1873)
MUSTON, Rev. Dr Alexis, The Israel of the Alps: A History of the Persecutions of the Waldenses (London, 1853)
PRO TORRE PELLICE, Guida Storico-turistica della Val Pellice, 3rd ed. (Torre Pellice, 1977)
TOURN, Giorgio, The Waldensians: the first 800 years (Turin, 1980)

The Italian Alps and Lakes
ANATI, Emmanuel, Valcamonica: 10,000 anni di storia (Brescia, 1982)
BAEDEKER, Karl, Northern Italy (Leipzig, 1913)
BAUM, Wilhelm, Storia dei Cimbri: origine, lingua e sviluppo deli insediamenti sudbavaresi nei Sette e Tredici Comuni in Italia Settentrionale (Landshut, 1983)
CANZIANI, Estella, Piemonte (Milan, 1917)
ECO, Umberto, Il Nome della Rosa (The Name of the Rose) (Sonzogno, 1980), tr. H. B. Jovanovich (London, 1983)
EDWARDS, Amelia B., Untrodden Peaks and Unfrequented Valleys: a midsummer ramble in the Dolomites (London, 1873)
LUND, Rev. T. W. M., The Lake of Como: its history, art and archaeology (London, 1910)
MANNI, P. E., I Campanili della Valsesia (Riva Valdobbia, 1979)
MANZONI, Alessandro, I Promessi Sposi (The Betrothed) (Milan, 1827), tr. Archibald Colquhoun (London, 1956)

The Roman Roads of Noricum
ALFÖLDY, Géza, The Provinces of the Roman Empire: Noricum (London, 1974)
BAEDEKER, Karl, The Eastern Alps (Leipzig, 1911)
CASSON, L., Travel in the Ancient World (London, 1974)
CHEVALLIER, R., Roman Roads, tr. N. H. Field (London, 1976)
HYDE, W. W., Roman Alpine Routes (Philadelphia, 1935)
ISTITUTO GIOVANNI XXIII, Biblioteca Sanctorum, pp. 938–9 'St Florian' (Rome, 1964)
MILTNER, Franz, Römerzeit in Österreichischen Landen (Innsbruck, 1948)
MOOSLEITNER, Fritz, Die Schnabelkanne vom Dürrnberg (Salzburg, 1985)
PLINY the Elder (Gaius Plinius Secundus), Natural History, tr. H. Rackham (London, 1969)
SITWELL, N. H. H., Roman Roads of Europe (London, 1981)

The Amber Route
BADEN PRITCHARD, H., Tramps in the Tyrol (London, 1874)
BATTISTI, Cesare, Il Trentino (Trent, 1917)
BRIARD, Jacques, The Bronze Age in Barbarian Europe (London, 1979)
CHIECO BIANCHI, Anna Maria, Il Museo Nazionale Atestino (Venice, 1985)
COLLESELLI, Franz, Companion Guide through the Museum of Tyrolean Folk Art (Innsbruck, 1986)
FERRANDI, Mario, L'Alto Adige nella Storia (Trent, 1972)
FORCHER, Michael, Il Tirolo: aspetti storici (Vienna, 1984)
FRANKENSTEIN, Baron Georg, Original Tyrolean Costumes (Vienna, 1937)
GRIESSMAIR, Hans, Das Südtiroler Volkskundemuseum in Dietenheim (Bozen, 1986)
GROHMAN, W. A. Baillie, Tyrol and the Tyrolese; the people and their land in their social, sporting and mountaineering aspects (London, 1876)
KREISEL, Heinrich, The Castles of Ludwig II of Bavaria (Darmstadt, c1960)
LUNZ, Reimo, Archäologie Südtirols, Teil 1; von den Jägern des Mesolithikums bis zum Ende des Weströmischen Reiches (Trent, 1981)
PERINI, Renato, Preistoria Trentina (Milan, 1984)
RICE, Patty C., Amber: the golden gem of the ages (New York, 1980)
TUCKETT, E., Pictures in Tyrol (London, 1867)

The Swiss Alps
BAEDEKER, Karl, Switzerland and the Adjacent Portions of Italy, Savoy and Tyrol (Leipzig, 1911)
BLACK, C. B., Guide to Switzerland and the Italian Lakes (Edinburgh, c1875)
DE BEER, Gavin, Travellers in Switzerland (London, 1949)
FLÜRLER, Niklaus, Switzerland (London, 1985)
MANNING, Rev. S., Swiss Pictures Drawn with Pen and Pencil (London, c1880)
MORRELL, Jemima, Miss Jemima's Swiss Journal; the first conducted tour of Switzerland (London, 1963)
SCHEUERMEIER, Paul, Bauernwerk in Italien, der Italienischen und rätoromanischen Schweiz (Zürich, 1943)
WHYMPER, Edward, Scrambles amongst the Alps in the Years 1860–69 (London, 1871)

INDEX